ERNESTINA SODI

DELIVER US
FROM EVIL

REPRESENTED BY:

DIANE STOCKWELL
GLOBO LIBROS LITERARY MANAGEMENT
402 EAST 64TH STREET, STE. 6C
NEW YORK, NY 10065
(212) 888-4655

ISBN: 1-59777-582-7
Library of Congress Cataloging-In-Publication Data Available

Book Design by: Sonia Fiore

Printed in Korea

Phoenix Books
9465 Wilshire Boulevard, Suite 315
Beverly Hills, CA 90212

10 9 8 7 6 5 4 3 2 1

FOR THALI

INTRODUCTION

I was kidnapped. One day, just an ordinary day like any other, a group of masked criminals took me hostage in the darkest, most sinister act of violence I have ever known. These men were deeply disturbed souls, trying to satisfy the most perverse desires, their actions reflecting a limitless need for power—that is the only reason I can think of that could explain why someone would hijack the life, the world and the values of another human being.

My captors insulted me, degraded me, and humiliated me. They denied me the most basic right of all human beings: freedom. And they tried to take away the one thing that is most sacred to all of us: life.

While I was kidnapped, I was locked up in a space no more than six feet by six feet, I was beaten and abused, and I was blindfolded for hours on end, every day. I was under constant threat and in a continual state of excruciating mental duress, enduring both psychological and sexual humiliation. Always under surveillance, I was ordered to be quiet as a mouse, as the constant drone of unbearably loud, shrill music played in the background all the time.

All of this took place in an environment that was completely foreign and terrifying to me. For several weeks, I was forced to live in a completely bizarre, surreal world where my captors treated me with callous indifference—that is, when they were not threatening to kill me—and yet, they also looked after me and tended to my basic needs.

I had no choice but to be docile and submissive. I was acutely aware that my life depended on my ability to be obedient and to tolerate the unspeakable madness I had been plunged into. Then, I learned the real meaning of isolation and loneliness. I learned the meaning of pain, as I struggled in silence to control the bitter tears that I shed every day. I was like an orphan, deprived of all affection and reduced to the status of an object, a thing to be bartered and traded.

The act of kidnapping is a terrifying drama that torments not only the victim, but their family and friends as well. It is a kind of torture that does not end upon release. Depriving people of their freedom is a heartless crime that reveals the rage, dissatisfaction and violence that exist in Mexico, and it is the innocent victims who inevitably pay the price for this stark reality. The ever-rising rate of kidnapping proves that the phenomenon is a social plague, and it underscores the need for real justice and respect for the guarantees purportedly granted us by law.

Kidnapping has become a flourishing industry, with no end in sight. It may touch anyone, at any time, for it is a crime committed against people regardless of gender, age, or social standing. Increasingly, the victims are women and children. Kidnapping is a crime that transforms a country into a place of fear, frustration and outrage. It is a violation that jeopardizes national security, and robs the government of its authority.

At the instant of capture, the victim embarks on a long road of panic and suffering, for it is an attack against life itself—physical, emotional, spiritual. The nightmare begins when the criminals seize the victims and announce that a kidnapping is taking place. In these first traumatic minutes, the victims struggle against their own thoughts and emotions. That struggle can last for days, weeks, months, or even years, as the victims try to overcome the recurring after-effects of their capture.

When you are kidnapped, the first thing you lose is your freedom. Soon after that, however, you also begin to lose your sense of reality, and your values. You begin to exist in a kind of void, fighting simply to survive this living nightmare, and then the moment inevitably arrives when you have to face the grim possibility that you could die. You become acutely aware of how fragile life is—and this is when the violence really gets to you, as you try to make sense of the two opposing worlds you now inhabit: the one you know and the one you have been thrust into. It is a crisis that sets off a spiritual battle inside of you, as you desperately seek some kind of meaning in your life.

After I was released, I spoke about my experience many times, and that allowed me to finally come to terms with my identity as a woman who had been victimized, a woman who had been rendered completely defenseless. It was a hard road, but it was the only one that helped me put my life back together and accept the hellish reality my captors had forced on me. It was a long, arduous path that compelled me to fight an infinite number of unforeseen battles that otherwise, I never would have had to confront. I suffered a great deal and shed many tears over it, but little by little, I was eventually able to accept the fact that no, none of what I had gone through was fair. It was just life—my life.

The kidnapping stole many things from me, most importantly time—precious time that belonged to me. I lost other things, too, many things. And yet now, in some way, that harrowing experience is something I have been able to leave behind, storing it away among my saddest memories, in a place deep inside of me where I keep all those life experiences that I have never been able to completely comprehend.

Today, here and now, I finally feel that I have triumphed. I look in the mirror and I see a survivor. I survived. And when I take a step back and think about it, everything I went through seems like something that happened to somebody else, some storybook heroine. I feel stronger every day, more and more eager to live, to make plans for the future, and most importantly to be here, writing this book—a book I never should have had to write in the first place. But, facts are facts, and these pages I write are my way of making sense of my experience, talking about what I learned, and sharing a few of the many realizations I made from having been the victim of a kidnapping.

First and foremost, I identify myself as a victim, but also as a survivor, and I hope that my story will give you a glimpse of what so many kidnapping victims have endured. This book is for all of them, for all those who died, who were raped, who lost their faith; for all those who are held captive at this very moment, and for those who will find themselves in that terrifying circumstance one day.

For them, and for myself, I offer you my story.

Thank you for reading these words.

THE PHASES OF
A KIDNAPPING

PHASE ONE: The moment of capture and the notification of the kidnapping.

PHASE TWO: The adaptation period and the beginning of the negotiation process.

PHASE THREE: The release, or the final outcome, the possibilities of which are many: a payment may be made in exchange for the victim's release; the victim may escape or be rescued; the victim's freedom may be secured via pressure or an exchange of some sort; or the victim may die, either in captivity or after the ransom payment has been made.

PHASE FOUR: The return. The victim is reunited with the family, and embarks on an extremely difficult period of adaptation and re-adjustment.

PHASE FIVE: The victim begins to work through the trauma. A time of significant life changes—emotional, social, professional, and financial.

PHASE ONE

THE MOMENT OF CAPTURE AND THE NOTIFICATION OF THE KIDNAPPING

SEPTEMBER 22, 2002: THE DAY OF THE KIDNAPPING

It is a great privilege to have lived a difficult life.
—Indira Gandhi

Fate always has a way of catching up with us. It is divine will, and there is no escaping it. I went where the path led me....

The pain in my hip has gotten worse; I seem to have a pinched nerve. Stretched out in my bed, I decide not to go. My sister, Laura Zapata, is performing in a play tonight, September 22, 2002, at 6:30, *The House of Bernarda Alba*, and she invited me to attend. No, no, I tell her, I don't feel very well. But a phone call from my friends convinces me to go, and this is the prelude to the lightning bolt that will strike me later on that evening....

"Titi," they say, using the nickname everyone calls me, "We're ready. Should we just meet you at the theater?" I hesitate, but in the end I make the decision that, unwittingly, would change my life forever. I say yes, alright, I'll go.

I get out of bed. The pain in my hip has intensified, and I take two aspirin and get into the shower. Have you ever had a hard time deciding what to wear? Tonight, I will pick out the clothes that I will wear to my kidnapping. How many people, I wonder, pick out the clothes they will die in? We never know, do we, if death will suddenly take us by surprise with a car accident, a heart attack, or a kidnapping, in that green dress, or those red shoes. In my case, the kidnappers catch me very well-dressed, in a tailored black suit, knee-high boots, and a pocketbook full of things I will never get the chance to use.

My friends and I watch the play, and when it's over we go backstage to congratulate my sister. She invites us out for a drink and some pleasant conversation among friends. The question of "who should I go with?" is a split-second decision.

"Titi, you come with me and they can follow us." As I open the door and get into my sister's rust-colored Volkswagon Jetta on the passenger side, I notice that the street is awfully quiet and dark.

Beside me in the driver's seat, my sister begins talking as she starts the car. "Titi, tell me, how do you think I did as Martirio?" She is talking about the character she played that evening. Laura is an intense woman with an accomplished career as an actress. She is the eldest of my four sisters, and she has always worked very hard. She has played some magnificent roles in the theater, on television and in films.

"I was amazed at how you made the character grow, she's much more mature, and…oh, will you look at that idiot, that's a garbage truck, of all things!"

"At this hour?" she says.

"I don't believe them, they've completely blocked off all the traffic. They're right in the middle of the street. Get into that lane. It's the only one that's moving."

There we are, five blocks away from the Teatro San Rafael, trying to get ourselves onto the Periférico, the highway that circles Mexico City.

Suddenly, I see a white van cut off the small car in front of us. After a few seconds, we hear tires screeching and another white van pulls up next to us, and then another one quickly moves into place behind us. My friends are now three cars away.

Abruptly, one of the doors of the van in front of us swings open, and a huge firearm—a rifle, or an assault weapon of some sort—emerges. A man dressed in black from head to toe jumps out and grabs the weapon from the open door. My stomach already in knots, the one thing that I can think of to say is, "Laura, get down, they're looking for a fight, they've got guns!"

I duck down. The last thing I see are two men dressed in black running toward us. One of them is clutching the gun, and the other one has a hammer in his hand. An instant later I hear the hammer smash through the car window next to my sister, Laura. My first reaction is to open the door, because I assume they want to steal the car. As I try to run from the car I see the two men seize my sister and shove her into the back seat of her own car. For a few endless moments, I remain frozen, and then the figures in black come after me: one of them tumbles over the hood of the car and grabs my arm, while the other one grabs me and presses the gun against my temple. Yanking me violently by the hair, he shoves me hard, pushing me down on my knees. Then he places the gun against my head. He starts to hit me with the barrel, in a series of sharp, fast blows. The panic that suddenly engulfs me is so overwhelming that my legs refuse to move, and my assailant begins to drag me along the ground, thinking that I am trying to resist him. But the truth is my body is simply frozen with fear. He pushes me into the front seat of my sister's car, in the middle with two men on either side of me. One is driving and the other one is pressed up against me in the passenger's seat. All of this transpires in a matter of seconds. Then I hear a panicked, frightened voice say, "Please, don't hurt them, they are ladies. Please."

"Shut up, son-of-a-bitch, and don't move or we'll shoot you," the voice of an older man barks back. Months later, I learn that my friend Fernando had actually gotten out of his car and attempted to intercede on our behalf.

At this point, time stands still and I enter another dimension. I feel as if I am somehow floating, and the only thing that brings me back to the moment is my heart, which is pounding at breakneck speed. They cover my face with one of their jackets. I crouch down, squished into that tiny space. In crisis situations like this, your physical self becomes everything. My breathing quickens from fear. Air, air! I try to remind myself that we must bring the outside world into the inside of our bodies, so that we can hold onto life. Adrenaline courses through my body, combined with a numbness and a strange, hot feeling, as if I've just taken a narcotic. My heart races on, and I feel as if it might jump right out of my body. My breathing grows more and more labored, and I'm almost afraid it will eventually stop, which would allow all of this to stop, too. This is fear. Real fear. I am afraid, I tell myself, and I repeat this mantra thinking about how fear is agitation produced by the imminence of danger, of something that may lead to pain, or death.

"Wall one, wall one. Forward."

When a kidnapping is set into motion, the car holding the victim is often flanked by other cars that serve as a kind of protective barrier, a "wall." This helps prevent other cars on the road from interfering in the process, and to clear the road and help the visibility of the main car— that is, the car with the victim inside.

"What is going on, you son-of-a-bitch? Don't be an idiot. I told you, move it!"

"Who is that following us? Shoot him, shoot him. Open fire now."

A gunshot goes off and suddenly my sister Laura's rust-colored Jetta comes to a halt. They yank us out of the car with our heads covered with jackets thrown over us, and through some gaps in the fabric I can just barely see that we have reached a street, a very dark alley where, not far off, a group of people are buying tamales. The men hustle us into a small white minivan, pushing my sister into the way-back and me into the back seat. On a two-way radio, one of the men calls out to his copilot:

"We got rid of the people tailing us. I tried to open fire on them with the machine gun but they're a bunch of lucky bastards because the thing got stuck and only one shot came out."

My sister is on the floor behind me and I'm in the back seat. We are two pieces of flesh, overflowing with adrenaline, afraid we may die at any minute, feeling as if they have severed our flow of energy with a pair of scissors. My foot is wedged in between the side door and the seat of the man next to me, who is slouching down low to avoid being seen. My foot hurts, but I can't move it. Soon it goes numb among the rest of the chaos that has erupted inside my body: my throat is dry, my heart is slamming into my chest, my sphincter is fluttering out of control, and my breathing…my breathing is heavier and heavier with every gasp of air.

A strong hand comes to rest on my shoulder.

"Don't worry, everything is all right."

"Wall two, move in closer, idiot. I said move it, damn it, someone can get through."

Oh my God, I think. Where on earth are they taking us? Suddenly, my mobile phone rings, and I know it's my daughter, calling to ask, "Where are you, Mommy?"

"Give me that fucking thing...someone was tailing us...who was it?"

"I don't know, sir."

"Shut your mouth."

I hand him my purse. Thinking that this is just a robbery, I tell him I have one thousand pesos in my wallet—about ninety dollars.

"A thousand pesos." He starts to laugh. "Give it to me and shut up."

Things go on like this for almost an hour, and we still have no idea where they are taking us, or what they are planning to do with us. This is when I begin to understand the meaning of what we often refer to, so casually, as "eternity."

My first reaction is complete and total bewilderment. Surprise is a kidnapper's best friend, and every victim's worst enemy. I am terrified that I will die: these men are armed. When they captured me, they had actually put a gun to my head. This can't be happening, I tell myself. This can't be! It's as if I were watching some kind of awful, unbelievable movie. Time has stopped...I feel as if I am flying, suspended in mid-air.... Ernestina, I tell myself, don't speak, don't cry, don't say anything...stay calm, everything is all right, stay calm, even the infinite has to come to an end sometime....

Fear strikes the heart, and brings with it pain, and this pain reminds us how valuable life is, as I begin to absorb, intellectually, this thing that is happening to me.

This pain works as a kind of alarm, both physical and spiritual, telling me how very dire this situation is, and placing me on high alert so that I can use every resource I possess to survive. Plato tells us that pain is produced when the harmonious balance of the elements that comprise a living being is threatened. This is exactly what I feel, this painful knowledge that I have been violently removed from my normal state of being. Everything happening to me is an attack against my will to live.

We come to a stop. I hear the sound of doors opening.

"Stay calm, stay calm, and keep quiet. Just follow us. And don't even think of uncovering your heads, no way. All right, calm, stay calm. Lower your head," someone says, taking me by the arm.

With the jacket over my head, I can't see anything except the ground beneath my feet: all I see is a series of spiral staircases. Twelve steps that I clumsily climb. The men lead me into a very dark room and sit me down on the edge of a bed, facing a wall, next to my sister. Our heads are still covered, we cannot see a thing. For an instant, we grab each other's hand and together we absorb the shock, the utter and total shock of what we are only beginning to endure. Suddenly, I hear a voice that I will never forget, a sharp, distorted voice that sounds like it belongs to an extraterrestrial in a science fiction movie. The voice says, "Do you know what's happened? This! This is a kidnapping!"

I squeeze my sister's hand, hard, and she does the same. My heart stops, as does hers, I am sure. I feel as if someone has just thrown a bucket of ice-cold water over us, completely paralyzing us.

"This is nothing personal. You have been kidnapped because of your brother-in-law's money, and we want five million dollars." They are talking about my other sister, who I will call the beauty queen, for that is what they call her for the duration of the kidnapping. She is married to a prominent Italian-American businessman in the United States. The kidnappers believe that, simply because we happen to be his sisters-in-law, he will pay our ransom.

Laura tells the man that we don't have that kind of money.

"I want your sister's phone number—the famous sister, the beauty queen."

Laura says she doesn't know it, but I tell them, "You can get it from my cell phone." They can't figure out how to retrieve the number, so they hand me the phone, pushing me toward the floor, my head still draped with the jacket. I try to turn on the phone, but realize that it is broken. They grab it from me, move away and then return, furious. In the middle of all this, another voice starts talking, again about my sister.

"We already spoke to the beauty queen, but she thought it was a joke and hung up on us. Another phone, hurry up, give us another phone. Where do you live? How many kids do you have? What are their names? What's your husband's name? How old are you?"

At this point, my sister explodes, and starts shouting at them.

"Why are you doing this to us? We're honest women, working women, mothers…we work ourselves to the bone to make a living. How dare you put us through this kind of shit? You're all a bunch of worthless…."

The man with the extraterrestrial voice, who appears to be the boss of the group, suddenly speaks up. The others call him the "Midget," and that is how I begin to identify him, too. He has somehow managed to distort his voice with either a machine, or possibly by swallowing his breath as he speaks.

"Now you listen to me, lady," he says, "we have not used any kind of vulgar language with you, so please don't speak to us that way again."

Despite everything, I seem to have remained calmer than my sister, so I squeeze her hand again and again to try to get her to calm down a bit.

Another voice interjects, "You're scared, that's all. Let me get you a drink. That will make you feel better."

Finally, it seems that they have made contact with someone in our family. My nephew, my sister's son, answers the first call. Poor baby, I can't even imagine what must be going through his mind as he takes in this horrible information, all alone, with no idea what to do…. They tell him to call his aunt, to tell her that it's true, and then they tell my nephew not to hang up or else there will be trouble.

Next, they give us some mezcal to drink, which does actually help me calm down a little.

The Midget comes back into the room and says, "Listen, Laura baby, we've contacted your ex-husband and he's demanding some kind of proof that you're alive. So I'm going to ask you a question: What's the name of your ex-husband's grandfather?"

"Jacinto," she replies.

"All right now, we're going to let your friend here go, we're going to get her ready and she can leave."

And my sister answers, "No! Please, don't let her go, she isn't my friend, she's my sister!"

My blood runs cold when I hear those words. And I think to myself, *why on earth would my sister tell them to keep me here?* Everything is a blur. Oh my God, I say over and over again, God, please, please have mercy on us.

"Is that true? Are you Laura and the beauty queen's sister?"

"Yes, sir."

"What is your last name?"

"My name is Ernestina Sodi Miranda."

"You have the same last names as the beauty queen."

"Yes, sir. That's right."

"Well, well...it looks like we've hit the jackpot! Ernestina, you're staying with us."

That is how it all began....

INITIAL CRISIS

Do what you fear and the fear will die.
—Jiddu Krishnamurti

In Phase One, the initial crisis, in those first minutes, hours, and days after finding out their loved ones have disappeared, family members live through the very worst kind of anxiety, chaos, confusion and fear. They usually begin a frantic search for their loved one's captors, but typically, things remain vague and unfocused until the first notification, that first contact from the captors. It may be a phone call, a letter, or a message informing the family that their relative has been kidnapped. The family immediately experiences a deluge of emotions. Naturally, they are terrified for the life and well-being of their loved one, but they may also feel rage, impotence, uncertainty, anxiety, guilt, sadness, bewilderment, abandonment, loss, and of course the hope that they will be able to locate their loved one and get him or her back.

Family members may react quite differently to this situation, depending on their individual temperaments. Some people are very good at expressing their feelings openly and clearly, while others are quiet and don't show their emotions, repressing them or simply refusing to accept that they are in fact deeply troubled by what has happened. Ultimately, it is very difficult to describe the effects of this type of experience because it is so profoundly shocking. Especially in the beginning, people are often unable to react naturally, and their true feelings may remain imbedded or suppressed as they subconsciously try to protect themselves from the terrible pain. This is what the initial crisis is all about.

As the days go by, the family members feel the absence of their loved one more and more acutely. As reality sinks in, the emotions grow even more intense, and people often have a difficult time assimilating the truth of the situation—that their loved one has disappeared or has been kidnapped. It is too much information, too overwhelmingly painful to digest all at once. They often don't know how to act, especially as they begin to receive conflicting advice from friends and acquaintances who have been through the same experience. Unfortunately, in Mexico kidnappings are not at all uncommon, and just about everyone has a theory or opinion on how to handle the problem. In the end, of course, every situation is unique, and in the first days and weeks it is excruciatingly difficult to try and decide on a course of action.

First and foremost, the family must accept the fact of the kidnapping, without pointing fingers or blaming anyone. At the very beginning, the most important thing is to focus on the problem and recognize that it will be a tremendous challenge to bring the victim home, safe and sound.

THE FAMILY

Love is a soul that dwells in two bodies;
a heart that dwells in two souls.
—Aristotle

"They just got in touch with us, and your grandson confirmed it. I don't know how they are. But listen, I've arranged for someone to pick you up and bring you here to New York, so that we can all put our heads together and figure out what to do."

And my daughters? My oldest daughter, Camila, who was sixteen years old at the time, found out that same night. After we were kidnapped, my friends went directly to my house and called my ex-husband. He was on his way over to the house when Camila realized that something was wrong, and asked what was going on. They told her straight out.

"Your mother was kidnapped with your Aunt Laura." They gave her the news very abruptly. They were probably in shock themselves, and they didn't stop to consider what might be the best way to break the news to Camila, who broke down immediately, scratching her arms and crying out, "Mamita, Mamita, no! No!" She was absolutely beside herself, so distraught that they considered injecting her with a sedative, but they waited. The news had leaked and everyone was talking about it, because it hadn't yet been confirmed whether it was true or not.

My younger daughter Marina was in school in France when I was kidnapped. While I was in captivity, I fantasized that when she called and I didn't answer, they would tell her I was participating in some kind of *Big Brother* reality show for writers, and that I was winning. But real life was different. Her father, Fernando, telephoned the school where she was studying and asked them not to let any calls go through, and to keep her from connecting to the Internet until he arrived there, so that he could explain everything to her himself. A relative immediately went to pick her up, because it was going to be very hard to keep the news from her, and there was no way she should be alone.

My sisters Federica and Gabriela were heartbroken and devastated, calling each other every so often to try and piece together what had happened. At first they thought maybe it was some kind of sick joke, wondering if it could really be a kidnapping.

After they had digested this initial information, my family quickly decided to pick one house where they would all stay, which would serve as the headquarters. It soon began to sink in that they would start receiving phone calls from our captors, and that they would have to start negotiating the price of our lives. For the first time ever, aside from Christmas vacations, everyone piled into the same house: ex-husbands, ex-sisters-in-law, nieces, nephews, friends, coworkers, and domestic staff, who continued to do their jobs despite the desperation and terror they felt, not knowing if they would soon be out of work, not knowing what would happen to them. As everyone arrived, they all looked at each other, wondering who would be the one they could all count on for a bit of calm and reassurance in that house, where everyone turned up with their eyes glazed over and their souls wracked with fear and dread. My house was the first place they gathered, and that is where their story begins.

And who stopped to think about my grandmother? My grandmother, my poor grandmother.

The story of our kidnapping began to make the evening news on the radio.

"It seems that two sisters of the singer and actress...were kidnapped yesterday. The victims are Laura Zapata, the talented and highly acclaimed actress, and her sister Ernestina Sodi."

Our pictures were plastered across the pages of all the newspapers, as they printed all kinds of theories about what had happened. Like bloodhounds, the TV, newspaper and magazine reporters located my house and parked themselves and their crews outside my door, staying there around the clock. Then came the phone calls...all the phone calls from our friends and acquaintances, wanting to know if it was true. They called and called, asking question after question after question. Although their intentions were good, this was in fact a problem. My family had to focus on the negotiations, and every time the phone was busy, they ran the risk of missing critical calls from the kidnappers. For this reason my family decided to move to another house and reduce the number of family members who would live out this kidnapping together, this horror story, a terrible journey into the unknown.

The lines of information and communication were cut, to a certain extent and with certain people, and this silence unfortunately created an atmosphere of anger and fear. The family nucleus closed ranks, and as its members dropped their everyday activities they entered another dimension. Friendships fell to the wayside. Their universe was reduced to the family on one side, and the kidnappers on the other. Everything was shrouded in uncertainty, and everyone was afraid—for themselves, and for us.

PHASE TWO

THE ADAPTATION PERIOD AND THE BEGINNING OF THE NEGOTIATION PROCESS

CAPTIVITY

If you don't have inner freedom, what other
kind of freedom can you hope to possess?
—Leonardo Da Vinci

Every kidnapping is unique, and each person faces this situation in his or her own way. So I would like to stress that while I will talk about many of the experiences I endured with my sister in captivity, she naturally has her own vision of this very difficult time we spent together.

One of the first things I remember Laura saying was something that cut to the depths of my soul.

"You know what? We have fallen into a horrible tragedy. Maybe the biggest tragedy of our lives."

"Why? Why?" I ask, over and over again. "And my daughters? My daughters...." As these things dawn on me, I break down in tears, the most heartbreaking tears I have ever shed. The sadness that fills me is unlike anything I have ever felt before. My daughters. Thinking of them is what hurts the most—more than thinking about myself, or my sisters, more than the situation I am in and the prospect of dying. I hurt for them.

The first night is terrifying. That is when it really hits me, that we are kidnapped, totally defenseless, in an environment dominated by violence, threats and fear.

Information...more information...this is what they want, they keep telling us. More information. Dream? Nightmare? Is this really, truly happening to me? People come and go. The sound of people brandishing guns is constant, ubiquitous: they do it to assert their power, their absolute authority over us.

My sister and I are sitting on the edge of the bed, with some sweatshirts thrown over our heads. One of the rules we had to strictly obey during this hell that was immediately drilled into us was to always quickly cover our faces whenever anyone knocked at the door. We were not to look at our captors for any reason, ever. If we saw them, we had the threat of death hanging over our heads. We used whatever we could quickly grab—a bath towel, the bedspread, a sheet. When they left and we were alone in the room again, we could take off whatever was covering our eyes.

"Don't go near the windows. If you go near the windows, we'll kill you."

The window, which is next to the bed, has bars and is covered with some rags and a blanket. The room is very small, around forty square feet, pitch black, with a bathroom and a closet without doors. There is one wooden bureau with two shelves, and on it sits a small, 14-inch television set. They tell us that it is to remain on, morning, noon and night, and that we are not allowed to touch it. This is when I realize that noise is the second weapon they are going to use to break us down. So much noise, both inside and outside, has a way of making everything—ideas, thoughts, feelings—very disorienting. And in fact, the method works: it is absolutely unbearable.

Soon, my hip starts to bother me again. The pain grows so strong that I can't walk anymore, and I have to drag my leg around to move at all. When I stop to think about it, I realize that "they" have taken away all my support—both moral and physical, since my legs are what hold me up. For all intents and purposes "they" have paralyzed me. But for some reason, just then I think about something Ernest Hemingway said: that man is not meant to be defeated. "A man," he once said, "can be destroyed but not defeated." And so that is what I repeat to myself: Ernestina, you cannot be defeated.

One of my captors knocks on the door and comes in, our heads are still covered.

"Tomorrow we'll take care of getting you what you need. Which one of you is bleeding?"

"Me," my sister replies.

"Do you want us to look at it? We'll get you gauze and alcohol if you want."

"No, thank you. I'll look after myself just fine," she says.

We shuffle into the bathroom, under orders that we are not to close the door. Laura washes her foot, which is bleeding from the glass that shattered when they broke through the car window with their hammer.

"Do you want anything else?"

I manage to squeak out one request. "Would you mind bringing me my cigarettes?" They comply immediately. In between sobs, I light a cigarette in the corner of the bathroom. Marvelous relief.

Neither of us wants to go to sleep in the bed. They place a video camera right in front of it so that they can keep an eye on us at all times. We ask permission to sleep on the floor, between the door and the bathroom. That way, at least, we don't feel as though we're being watched. I hear one of them say, "These old ladies are nuts. They want to sleep on the floor."

They give us a couple of pillows, black Oriental-style pillows with a flower design on one side. On these revolting cushions I lay my head. Finally, I take off the sweatshirt that has been wrapped around my head and I can see through the darkness, through the glow of the television screen, up to the ceiling. As I look up, around the light I can make out some kind of decorative touch on the ceiling that looks like a Star of David, and the moldings around it. In front of me there is a picture of Christ in a light-blue tunic, holding out his arms, with a ray of light emanating from his hands. He looks at me with a sweet smile on his face. *My God, are you here with me?* I ask myself for the first time.

My sister and I speak softly to one another.

"What are we going to do?" we ask, as we listen to the sounds of dogs barking, guns clicking, and cars speeding past. And the night, the awful, hateful night....

The next morning, I wake up and try to get to my feet, but it isn't easy. I drag myself to the bathroom and begin to vomit from the constant nausea brought on by this awful situation, this awful place. It rises up from somewhere deep inside of me. Every fifteen minutes or so, I vomit again. I vomit green bile.

"I don't know how you managed to fall asleep," my sister says.

I don't know, either. Maybe the shock was so overwhelming that the only thing my body knew how to do was disconnect. It makes me think that maybe we are made of the same thing dreams are made of, and that our brief lives are, in fact, part of a dream.

According to Laura, I actually snored that first night.

Someone knocks at the door. We quickly cover our heads and he enters the room.

"My name is Rudy. I'm going to take care of you. Tell me what you need. First of all I'm going to get you some pants, so that you'll be more comfortable. Here's your breakfast." He sets it down and leaves. Fruit and orange juice. I drag myself over to the bathroom, to vomit again. It tastes bitter, just like everything.

At some point I tell my sister that I've read about kidnappings, and that this may drag on for a long time. Maybe three, even four months. She tells me to be quiet, not to talk about those things. But I know it: we may be in for a very, very long haul. From what little I know about kidnappings, I know that it involves a period of negotiation, and that the criminals will try to get the maximum amount of money they can by pressuring the family until they break.

The kidnappers are well-versed in developing a kind of Pavlovian response in their captives. They bring us food that they know is the right kind of food for the circumstances we're in: today, chicken broth and herbal tea, to soothe the bile. I manage to swallow three spoonfuls of the broth. To my surprise it tastes quite good, but I am unable to get down any more.

On Wednesday, September 25, we wake up to a big commotion in the house.

"Now we're really fucked!" we can hear one of them say.

"What are those goddamn policemen doing out front?"

"I don't know, someone said something about a drug raid. But if they come in here, I'll get in the doorway, you go inside, and open fire on them in there, and from then on it's every man for himself."

"Should I kill them?"

"That's what I said. Yes, fire at them and then the fucking game starts. Then we'll see what those cops are made of."

As I listen to them talk, my stomach tightens into a knot again and I try to control my heart, which is pounding faster than ever, as a burning heat starts to rise inside of me.

"Oh my God, oh my God, don't let them come in! God, please don't let them come in! I don't want to die, not like this!" This goes on for two hours. At some point, they threaten to separate us.

Then someone comes in the room and says, "We're going to have to change your rooms, maybe move you to a new house. It's too dangerous here."

"Wait a minute, you're not Rudy, you're someone else," I say.

"I'm Rudy." But his voice and presence are different. The first Rudy walks with a heavy, lumbering stride, smells like old olive oil, and from the way he talks I can tell he is somewhat uneducated—it almost sounds as if he has trouble speaking Spanish, as if he gets confused between Spanish and some other native dialect. Rudy #2 is lighter on his feet, and I can tell from his voice that he's much younger. He smells, unlike Rudy #1, like soap and he's somewhat educated. These are the things that happen when you can't see. Your other senses grow sharper; with your nose and your ears, you perceive things that might otherwise escape you.

From that day on, we understand that there are two Rudys; for that reason we call one of them Rudy and the other one Romeo.

Around mid-day they move us to a room on the third floor of the house. It is dark, though not as dark as the first room; the light somehow manages to slip in through a crack. The television is again left on, blaring all the time, and the radio is too; it blasts loud Mexican music day and night. It is so irritating that I can't help but wonder if their neighbors don't complain constantly about the unbearable music that they blast from the house. In the middle of this racket I actually manage to hear a snippet of the TV news and that's when I hear someone announce that "Laura Zapata and her sister Ernestina Sodi have disappeared, which may mean that they have been the victims of a kidnapping, though the family has not yet filed any report with the police." I hear a whistle, and then someone knocks on the door. By now we have learned that a knock on the door means that we are to cover our heads with whatever we can grab; today, we use dirty towels from the bathroom.

They come inside and warn us that every time the news comes on we have to change channels. They don't want to have to kill us or hurt us, they say, but if we don't obey their orders they will have no other choice but to do one of the two. Then they announce that we are going to be moved to another house, and that they plan to separate us. My sister starts to cry and begs them not to, promising the men that we'll behave ourselves.

When they move us to another room, the man leading me around tells me that we have permission to take baths. He has noticed that I smell—like sweat, like adrenaline, fear, captivity and vomit. He's right to point it out; even I can't stand myself anymore. And so they give me a pair of old pants, shampoo and soap. My sister begs them not to separate us and wraps her arms around my waist. One of the men takes me by the hand to lead the way to the bathroom. A strange sensation runs through my body right then; his hands are soft, warm, and he guides me along tenderly. Once we're alone in the bathroom, I tell my sister, "You know, when that guy held my hand it felt warm, nice."

"Oh, Titi," she says, calling me by my nickname. "None of these delinquents have a shred of warmth in them; they're criminals, all of them."

But inside, I feel she's wrong; that one man, he isn't so bad. I don't think he has blood on his hands.

In that first house, we are given breakfast at around nine in the morning, usually apples and cereal. We always eat sitting on the floor. At lunchtime they serve us things like beef stew, chicken broth, spaghetti *a la poblana*, and breaded chicken cutlets. At night, usually around 8 o'clock, we are given *sincronizadas* with ham-and-cheese tortillas. Oddly enough, the food is very tasty, maybe even homemade.

On the third day, one of the kidnappers knocks and comes in. He tells us that they are going to move us that evening, and he gives us a couple of plastic bags for our things. It's strange, of course, because in that unreal place, "our things" are nothing more than what they have given us: creams and toothbrushes and a couple of sweatshirts. Just before we go to the bathroom to shower, they take all our jewelry and all the clothing we were wearing when they captured us. My sister, though, manages to hang onto a beautiful ring with eight tiny diamonds, by stuffing it in her bra. Then she turns to me and says, "Titi, I can't give these monsters my ring. I'm going to put it in my bra; they'll never know it's there." At some point later on, I don't remember exactly when, she hides it in a bottle of shampoo.

The sun goes down and things start to happen. People moving around, footsteps, voices. And there we are, not knowing if this is going to be the hour of our death—if they are taking us to some other city or town, or if they're going to throw us in a ditch somewhere. We don't know anything. With towels draped over our heads, they guide us out the door to somewhere; God only knows where. And then they hand us cotton balls. We are to place them over our eyes, which are already pressed shut, and then they tie the blindfolds around our heads. My feeling about this is oddly mixed, as I idly wonder if I am better off this way, unable to see the hell that I am living in, cut off and totally helpless without my sight, one of my five precious senses.

"Is it too tight?"

"No, sir."

"Whenever I tell you that we're going to blindfold you, always make sure to have the cotton balls ready. Understood?"

"Yes, sir."

"Miss Laura, please come with us."

My sister begins to tremble and grabs my hand, but they separate us, and a pit forms in my stomach yet again. This is the first time during this ordeal that they have separated us, two blood sisters, two bleeding souls, two mothers without their children, two confidantes, scared to death.

First they bring my sister downstairs and sit her down in the back of a van with no seats. Then they place me next to her, and cover us with a pile of blankets. My sister and I can only communicate with each other through our feet. We tremble. This particular experience is one of the most difficult to overcome, to put behind me: blindfolded, caged, smothered by blankets, and the threat of death constantly hanging over me.

We reach the second house. It only took about five minutes to get there. This second house must be very close to the first one. Just like before, our room is on a second floor. It's a little bigger than the previous room, and it has a bathroom and an open closet. The window, like before, has bars and is also covered with dark curtains, shutting out all light except for what manages to filter through a tiny hole, which lets me know when the sun is out. In the middle of the room sits a king-size bed...and from then on, two lost souls ripped out of the world they once knew.

COEXISTENCE

LIFE WITH THE KIDNAPPERS BEGINS

Men are moved by two levers only: fear and self-interest.
—Napoleon Bonaparte

K idnapping is an act that deprives a person or group of people of their freedom, normally lasting a finite period of time, with the aim of collecting a ransom or gaining some kind of leverage in politics or the media. People who carry out kidnappings are known as kidnappers.

The Spanish word for kidnapping is *secuestro*. The English cognate of this word, *sequester*, isn't quite a synonym but it comes very close. Etymologically speaking, both words find their root in the Latin *sequestrare*, "to take control of a person with the intent to demand a sum of money, or to detain someone illegally." In ancient times, kidnapping was also called *plagio* in Spanish, which means "fishing net." (*Fundación País Libre, 1999*)

Kidnapping is a violation of human rights that also infringes upon the freedom, integrity and peace of the families of the victims of this crime. It is also a violation of articles 1, 3, 5, and 9 of the Universal Declaration of Human Rights, adopted and so declared by the General Assembly of the United Nations in Resolution 217(a) (iii) on December 10, 1948, and still in effect. As such, the act of kidnapping is defined as something that affects not only the victim but his or her entire family, given that they are subjected to what psychologists in the field of grief counseling refer to as "suspended death," which is the very same agony caused by kidnapping, and which legal scholars deem "a loss of freedom." (*Fondelibertad*)

In general, the kidnappers' work begins by closely watching the daily activities and patterns of their victims for several days. They learn their victims' traffic routes and everyday schedules, which helps them to effectively carry out their plans. Ninety percent of kidnappings are executed either when the victims are traveling by car through desolate areas (with little or no pedestrian traffic) or when they enter or leave their homes. When the kidnapping is carried out by an organization that specializes solely in this type of crime, the members tend to operate in cells, dividing the responsibilities among themselves. For example, one cell may focus exclusively on negotiating with the victim's family over the phone to demand a ransom. Others are charged with feeding and guarding the victims, while others are only involved at the moment of intercepting and capturing their victims and delivering them to their place of captivity which, incidentally, can often change during the course of a kidnapping in order to confuse the authorities, in the event that an investigation is launched to locate the victim.

The following are the subgroups typically found in kidnapping organizations:

The *initiator* is the person who facilitates the contacts, acquires the (usually stolen) vehicle, and secures the house that will be used to house the hostage. The initiator also procures the weapons necessary for the operation and gains access into the victim's social sphere in order to gather as much information as possible before the kidnapping actually takes place.

The *lavaperros* (literally, dog-washers) are those members of the group who are responsible for "lifting" the victims—that is, physically capturing them and bringing them into captivity. One kidnapping operation usually requires several of them. Within the kidnapping world, they are the most disposable people involved, because they tend to have little regard for life, whether it be their victims' lives or their own.

The *custodians* are the people who take care of the hostages. In general three custodians suffice to look after one hostage, but this depends on the organization. Women may be involved who are in charge of feeding the victims. These people are also responsible for providing the proof to demonstrate to the victims' families that their loved ones are in fact alive. To this end, they use intimidation and threats to force the victim to answer questions, write letters or appear in videos, which are then transmitted to the family members. The custodian must also attend to the needs of the victims to avoid any unexpected circumstances during the period of captivity.

The *negotiator*, as the name suggests, is the person in charge of contacting the family, pressuring them psychologically, and devising a plan for the ransom payment. The negotiator generally holds a high position in the hierarchy of the kidnapping organization.

KIDNAPPING NEGOTIATIONS

A family attempting to rescue their loved one from a kidnapping will most likely have to go through this very difficult process. The first step is confirming that the person in captivity is, in fact, their loved one. To this end, the family must demand from the negotiator some kind of irrefutable proof that their family member is indeed being held captive by the negotiator's group, and that he or she is still alive. This is critical, because in some cases several groups have claimed to have kidnapped the same victim. One typical method of proving the authenticity of a kidnapping is by taking a photograph of the victim holding the morning newspaper, or a magazine published within their power to get it.

In my case, my family did exactly the right thing: they went directly to the Mexican Attorney General's office to file a kidnapping report. Once this was done, their case was brought to the attention of the Agencia Federal de Investigación (AFI, Federal Investigation Agency) and the Subprocuraduría de Investigación Especializada en Delincuencia Organizada (SIEDO,

Deputy Attorney General for Specialized Investigations in Organized Crime), both of which investigate kidnapping cases. Experts in this topic, the people at the SIEDO and AFI work to educate and help family members carry out a successful negotiation with kidnappers. While they are not permitted to negotiate directly on behalf of the family, they do help prepare the negotiator the family has chosen, so that he or she knows exactly how to handle the back-and-forth of the negotiation process. These professionals are intimately familiar with the kidnappers' standard operating procedures and their mindset.

Of course, it goes without saying that this is the most perverse game imaginable, because the kidnappers generally know that families are being advised by the AFI, even though they pretend that they don't. The AFI agents, for their part, know how to handle the psychological element as well as the timing factor with these criminals. Naturally, every case is different, and some cases do end up with the victim's assassination due to poor negotiation.

In the third step, the family's negotiator must somehow make the kidnappers understand that all that glitters is not gold, and that it is really going to be very hard to come up with the sum they are demanding. During this phase, the family must try to get the kidnappers to budge, even just a little bit, in their demands. The best way to do this is by showing them debts, IOUs, documents proving that properties are owned by a company or several business partners. The main idea in all of this is to convince the captors that everything they see is not necessarily the property of the victim or the victim's family. This, in the end, is what will convince the captors to lower their ransom demand and begin bargaining. At the same time, this tactic has the effect of prolonging the negotiation and exhausting the kidnappers a bit. The most important thing of all here is to reinforce the idea that turning properties into cash is not so simple. This may also serve to erode their business in the end: if they know or think that cash is easily procured, they are likely to kidnap again and again and again. Nevertheless, there is a very delicate balance that the family has to maintain here, because a very drawn-out negotiation process naturally places the victim under an excruciating level of physical and mental duress.

Throughout the entire negotiation process, which generally transpires over a series of phone calls, the family must also continue to demand proof that the victim is still alive. The best kind of negotiator is able to establish an atmosphere of trust and good faith, so that the kidnappers see themselves as friends helping to solve a problem. When this tactic is employed well, captors are far less inclined to switch negotiators in the middle of the process, which inevitably slows things down and sabotages any previous ground rules or conditions agreed upon by both sides.

Any family that finds itself in this situation should consider very carefully the relationship it wants to have with the authorities. In our case, reporting it to SIEDO and AFI was the right decision. A great many families in

Mexico have chosen not to report kidnappings to the appropriate authorities. But with this book I would like to emphasize how important it is to report these crimes, to create a culture of reporting it immediately. If there is no report, there is no crime to investigate or punish.

Our first night in the new safe-house is even more nerve-wracking than before. The sound of guns being cocked is our eternal background noise, along with the sound of bullets hitting the floor outside our room. We can also hear people sniffing very loudly and then sneezing violently.

"There's no more powder left, man," we hear one of the men say.

"Oh, my God," says my sister. "These guys are drugged out...and look, there are bullet holes in the wall! And did you see this rug? That's scrubbed-out blood there. I think they killed someone in here...."

With every word my sister utters I panic a little more, so much so that I have to put up a mental barrier, and I tell myself over and over, *You can't think negatively. You have to be positive. Positive. It's the only way you're going to get out of here.*

All your senses are heightened when you are kidnapped. The sounds of the safe house become part of your breath, the most intimate element of your life. Between six and seven in the morning, for example, we can hear the sound of one vendor yelling, "Gas! Gas!" and then someone else selling forty oranges for ten pesos. I listen to the birds singing. Rudy comes in and turns the television volume up. Way up. At the same time, someone outside the room turns on a radio, playing music by Alejandro Fernández. Our captors tend to play Mexican *ranchera* music almost incessantly, especially one particular song, "*El abandonado*"—the abandoned one.

For the first time, they turn off the television. The night, as black as our spirits, seems to fold in on us. Soon, we begin hearing terrifying noises that make us look up; it sounds as if dogs are racing across the roof, dragging their chains. My self-defense instincts respond immediately, disconnecting me physically so that I can rest, although my subconscious remains on high alert. I sleep next to the door, and despite my concentrated efforts to control my fear I can't help thinking that they might open the door at any moment and kill us. If that happens, the first bullet will be for me. We can hear them standing guard outside our door; one of the men actually sleeps lying down across the threshold. In the beginning we can tell that they have trouble falling asleep too, but as the days go by some of them actually start snoring, which in turn makes it even harder for us to sleep.

There's a knock at the door. We cover our heads with blankets so we can't see. "Good morning," Rudy says as he comes in. After he turns the television on he starts cleaning and sweeping the room.

"Boy does it stink in here, it's so humid," he says, opening a window. This is the first and only time of the day when we are granted fresh air, though we are not allowed to enjoy it since we have to cover ourselves whenever they come in.

"I brought you fruit and juice. What else do you need?"

Days earlier they had given me an anti-inflammatory medicine called Lonol, and an antacid for my sister. The Lonol helps alleviate the pain in my hip and prevent the full onset of a strange paralysis that has begun to affect part of my face.

"Titi, what's wrong with your face?"

We don't have a mirror; all I have are my sister's eyes. I touch my face and suddenly I notice a slight tickle and then a definite numbness, and I can also feel that the right-hand side of my mouth doesn't respond. I am really scared when I realize that I can't move my right eyebrow, and when I touch the right side of my nose, I don't feel a thing. But something inside of me rebels against all this. *Nothing is wrong with me*, I tell myself. *I am part of God and my spirit is strong. There is nothing the matter with me. I am not sick and my face is perfectly normal.*

I feel certain that God sees me as a survivor, and I cannot allow my body to defeat my will to remain strong, solid, and whole. I apply a bit of the Lonol to my face and leg, and I give myself massages to revive that part of me that has weakened. Little by little, never losing my faith or my will, I am able to walk with difficulty, and to "lift" the troubled half of my face back into place, and even feel it a bit. To calm the anxiety I still feel, and to help convince myself that everything is under control, I turn to my sister and ask, "Laura, is it better now?"

"No," she replies. "Your right eye is still lopsided."

"That's all I need right now; a paralyzed face. I won't let it happen, I won't, I won't...."

Coexistence settles in sooner or later. Time and captivity have a way of forcing us to adapt to the difficult circumstances of the kidnapping. As I envision the kidnappers in my many idle moments I feel the need to give them form, age, height; I need to imagine how they look. *They are human beings, just like me*, I tell myself. This is what I have to do to hang onto my sanity; otherwise I will feel that I am dealing with ghosts. My imagination takes me to places that I never knew existed. How can you visualize someone just on the basis of a voice? I ask myself. In the end, of course, it is more than just a physical shape that I am trying to fashion in my mind's eye; it is a soul— a soul worn thin by bad deeds, impervious to other people's pain, without remorse or fear of God.

The group of kidnappers is large, but the ones that make the strongest impression on me through my senses (other than sight) are:

The Midget: He seems to be the head of the group at the house. When I say "head" I mean that he is the person who is exclusively in charge of a specific cell. This particular man is especially perverse; he is truly evil. I can tell he is short, around fifty years old, maybe older. He never sleeps in the safe house, but he comes by around every third day to check up on things. Each and every visit he makes strikes terror into my heart. He is abusive, yells a lot and barks orders at his men, either to hit me, to scare me, or not to feed me. This is a man filled with rage, hatred and blind fury, a man who is determined to make everyone around him pay for the suffering that he himself has surely endured.

The Northerner: This man, I can tell, outranks the Midget. He pays us a visit only once, and every one of us fears his presence, even the kidnappers. He observes everyone's activities, and the men have to hand him reports on what has been going on at the house. I think he is around forty-five years old, and his energy is even blacker than the Midget's. You can smell the dead people emanating off of him. From the bits of conversation I can catch, I get the sense that he has some kind of relationship with the police and the ex-bureaucrats who still wield some power in Mexico. I am sure he is involved in drug trafficking, as well.

Rudy: A thin, tough young man about twenty-five years old. A few times I manage to catch a glimpse of his hands: they are bony, dark-skinned, and leathery. One day he admits that he is related to Daniel Arizmendi, one of the greatest and bloodiest kidnappers in Mexican history, known by the nickname of *"Mocha Orejas,"* the ear-clipper, because of his trademark: he always mutilated the ear of his victim. Rudy is a caretaker of sorts and his job is to bring us food, look after us, and clean the room every day. He tells us that the second safe house belongs to him. Extremely intelligent and astute, he also appears to be addicted to marijuana.

Romeo: A heavy-set young man, about twenty-six years old, with big green eyes—that is, at least, how he describes them to us. Every so often I manage to sneak a peek from under the blankets we cover ourselves with, and I can see his shoes. They are stylish and expensive, as are his clothes, from what I can tell. He tells me he shops at Zara. Very romantic, he is a man of slightly nobler sentiments than the others, and falls in love easily. But he is also more schizophrenic, more mentally disturbed, violent, and unpredictable than the others. His job is to obtain the money to feed everyone in the safe house, and to pay the gas, light, and telephone bills. He doesn't sleep at the house every night; he comes and goes. When they free my sister, he decides to stay every day until they let me go.

Pancho: About thirty-five years old, Pancho is big and burly. He says he is married with two children, and claims to be the owner of the first safe house where, in fact, we did spot children's toys and things. Rough voice. A total alcoholic, he drinks every day and on the weekends we can hear him vomiting and complaining about his hangovers.

He is always the one to offer us alcohol. His job is to look after the caretaker and the gunmen. Occasionally he makes the phone calls to our family members.

Cuquito: A very young man, no older than fifteen. He hardly ever talks; he is the designated triggerman. Every so often (like the day they bring me outside to take in a little sun), I bump into him, because I am always blindfolded. That is when I ask him his name, and he tells me that he is called Cuquito. He is the one who most often calls me "Sodi."

There is another man I never exchange a word with, though I can feel his presence. And every so often I can make out the sound of women's voices, but they never come very close.

The Midget, in my mind, is like Pancho's father. Pancho and Romeo are friends—they met each other stealing cars, and Pancho brought Romeo into this line of work. They are always telling us there is no such thing as friendship among kidnappers, that they never reveal their real names, much less where they live, to one another. And they also talk about how they operate in cells, and there are many, many cells in the organized crime world. The men that negotiate don't know the men that take care of us, and the ones that carry out the kidnapping don't know the first thing about the other men. They all have cell phones that they use exclusively for their kidnappings, and they call each other by nicknames without ever really knowing who they're working with. They operate according to a whole series of rules that they cannot break under any circumstances because a tiny mistake could cost them their lives, and not just their own lives, either. Every one of them knows that if something goes wrong, their bosses will kill every last member of their families. Each cell has a specific function, but there is, of course, a big boss out there somewhere. Nobody knows him, but he has the last word, he makes all the final decisions. I feel absolutely certain that this man works within the ranks of the police, or the government. And I say this because I always hear the men saying that the bosses are going to be protected no matter what, and that our blood would run cold if we ever found out which of our public servants were involved in this type of thing. Within their cell, our captors respect one another, and they seem to get along reasonably well in general, with the exception of a few crises that we all go through together.

I call our caretaker Rudy, who asks us to call him by that name. He is gritty, tough, young, and uneducated but as I mentioned before he is sharp and very suspicious. I picture him with dark skin and dark hair, with the sharp eyes of an eagle. He takes drugs three or four times a day. He also feeds drugs to the Dobermans they keep upstairs.

"Those wild beasts are called Godzilla and Kikon, and we keep them around just in case you try to escape— they won't let you out of here alive. During the day they sleep because every time I smoke pot I blow the smoke their way and they get nice and stoned, but at night they start bugging us for pot and I don't give it to them, which gets them real mad; so mad that they'd kill someone if I let them. Anyway, this house is like a bunker—there's a fence around the entire place, and there are weapons all over the place. We've got powder, guns, pistols, AK-47s, rifles and grenades. If the police ever come and surround the place, we'll just open a grenade and we'll blow everyone up, including you, because we'd rather die than go to jail."

This information sends us into a state of near-constant panic. One afternoon we hear a helicopter flying overhead and all we can do is cry and pray to God that they don't find us. Ironic as it may seem, our greatest fear is that the police will come and get us.

"Don't cry. That gets us nervous, and then we might lose our patience," they tell us. One more right they take away from us: the right to cry. Crying is the way our bodies assimilate and drain the ache we feel in our hearts. What is it about the exquisite machine that is the body, that when we feel anxiety or fear or sadness we produce a salty liquid that must be expelled uncontrollably from our eyes? Why salty? Is that the taste of pain?

Rudy is the lowest in the pecking order of the cell, and the worst paid—according to him at least. He comes into our room every morning, and the first thing he does is turn on the cartoons on television, always as loud as possible. Laura and I obediently cover ourselves with the blanket before he comes in, and he sits by our feet, laughing and talking for hours on end.

"Boy, if this bed could talk would you ever hear some stories.... You know, I fell in love with the Princess. Hey Sodi, what if you wrote the story, because you're a writer, aren't you? Would you write my story?"

"Yes," I tell him.

"Well, I'd tell you about how I fell in love with a girl we kidnapped and how that's the only thing that keeps me alive. She has a voice like the little girls from the Powerpuff Girls; the loudest one, the blonde one. But the Princess wasn't blonde. The little Princess had dark hair, real skinny but real pretty, too. She was very lonely and I spent a lot of time with her. One day I blindfolded her and then I kissed her."

"No, that can't be true," I say to him. "That's too crazy to be true."

"I'm telling you, it's true. Nothing happened. But my little Princess is my one reason for living. I don't want to keep on doing this. If I wrote a book it would be called 'The Song of the Bird.' First because I want to fly, fly like a bird and then because I want to write about everything that burns me up inside. I love music, you know, because every song has some kind of life experience in it, you know? Every time I hear something that reminds me of when I was a little kid, I feel that vibration of my life, it's like trapped there. Our lives are all there in the music, really.... Anyway, I've got to go now."

Rudy walks away, limping—those unmistakable footsteps that could only be his. As he leaves we hear him let out a great big sigh, the sigh of someone who, after all is said and done, is still just a man.

After I was released I actually met "the Princess," and I feel lucky to be able to call her my friend today. The SIEDO and AFI agents did an excellent job: after my kidnapping was reported, I gave them a detailed description of everything that had happened, and they told me that there was indeed a woman who had told them that one of her captors had called her "the princess." The agents decided that she and I should meet, because our descriptions—of the room, the noises, the food and most importantly the captors—were identical. One afternoon, the Princess came over to my house and, never having laid eyes on each other, we hugged and hugged, and then we cried and cried for several hours after that eternal embrace, and finally when we separated we looked in each other's eyes and a friendship was born.

One afternoon, I tell my sister, "Laura, take a shower, please! It will do you good. You need it; it will give you energy, and this room already smells bad enough without us making it worse."

I shower first, and my sister goes in after me. We are just getting dressed when they tap on the door. The two of us dutifully walk over to the bed and throw a blanket over our heads. All the men come into the room, nervous because their big boss, the one who calls himself the Northerner, has arrived.

"All right. Sit down facing the wall with the blanket over you."

We sit down at the edge of the bed, our legs pressed up between the bed and the wall, the blanket covering us entirely, the adrenaline coursing through us; that hateful adrenaline that makes the body feel hot and the heart pound like a hammer. This sensation is a daily one for us, and there is always something that sets it off. This time it's something big. My senses heighten with each passing second. Right now I feel that this man is the most vile murderer I have ever come across in my life.

"Well, well, look what we have here."

With one stride, the Northerner flops down on the bed, lying next to us; two lumps facing the wall and a big, hulking body just inches from our hips, our bodies almost touching.

"So...they tell me the two of you behave your-selves, that you don't cause any trouble. And you, Laurita, how come you cry so much?" A pause. "I'm talking to you, answer me."

"Yes, sir."

"Well, answer me."

"For my children."

"'My children,' yeah right. My father never thought about us. He was a policeman, one of the tough ones, always had a pistol on him. Hey kids, get lost, I'm in a good mood today, I want to have a little chat...."

The other kidnappers leave the room.

"That son-of-a-bitch, he was a real bastard with my mother, always hitting her, and not just her, either. Once he broke a chair over my back. Goddamn old bastard, I hate him. He ruined my back. He was always getting drunk, humiliating us, with words and with his fists. Whenever he got like that he would start threatening me with his gun, and he'd put it against our heads or between our legs. I've got nine brothers, and four of us work in this business, and we've got some other interests, too."

As the man talks on and on, my sister and I sweat like we've never sweat in all our lives, the blanket still covering us.

"Once my old man tortured my little brother...just when he was about to kill the kid I stepped in and for the first time in my life my father and I faced each other like two men, for real. And let me tell you, it feels rotten, because a son is supposed to respect his father and everything. But if I didn't hit him or do something he was going to kill my brother, my favorite little brother. Oh, my poor mother, she doesn't have any idea what kind of kids she gave birth to.... Two of them are with God now. One more is in jail, and the rest of us out here living this life just for fun.... You know what, Laurita? I've seen you on TV.... You're a real tough broad, aren't you?"

"No, sir, those are just the characters I play."

"Don't play innocent with me, I know you can be damn stubborn when you want to, but you're also real cute...."

My sister and I hold hands and squeeze because we feel the bed start to shake. A few long seconds go by before it dawns on us that this man is masturbating. Then he says,

"Oh, Laurita, you're so hot, you don't know how much I like it when old ladies like you get all wild."

The bed shakes and creaks more and more and Laura and I just sit there, waiting for something terrible to happen—specifically, that this man is going to get so aroused that he's going to try and rape us.

"Oh, Laura, Laura, you're so hot…. Yes, like that, like that…. Mmm, that's nice, that's it, yes, yes…." My sister and I cry in silence. Bathed in perspiration we can feel the water flow from our eyes and our bodies. Finally the man gets up and wipes himself off with our blanket, leaving us with his revolting smell.

"All right, now, I hope you keep behaving like you have so far. I don't know if I'm going to come back but I want to make one thing clear: if you don't cooperate you won't see your children ever again. Or even simpler: you won't ever see the sun again." Kicking the door open, he leaves the room and we immediately remove the stinking blanket. As I look at my sister I see what she surely sees in me: the devastating image of a woman with her hair plastered against her forehead with sweat, and a crazed look in her eyes, trying hard to keep from going completely mad in a room that smells like humidity and semen, trying to survive as she asks herself what life is all about, and how it is possible that human beings come to do these things.

I get to thinking about how Mexicans have been carrying this bottled-up rage inside of them ever since the conquest, when we were defeated…. Almost all the indigenous women were raped by the Spanish conquerors, and the result of those unions was a new race of Mexicans that were born only to be rejected by their mothers, who felt stung by the humiliation of having to carry these unwanted children in their wombs, their spirits...and so the story goes. The conquerors imposed their religion and their customs on the native people, who were in fact the real possessors of everything. And yet they, the indigenous people, were the ones who were punished the most, enslaved by the powerful and wealthy foreigners who took their land, their most valuable possession.

The criminals who have kidnapped me exhibit a frighteningly fierce kind of rage—a rage against life, against their fellow man, against society in general. Sitting there, I start to get the feeling that all of this is part of an ancestral hatred that has grown and deepened over the centuries, creating monsters in the bodies of men who hate themselves, their parents and the world. More than a transaction involving money, it seems that kidnapping is an attempt to avenge the massive differences that exist in Mexico, between the haves and the have-nots. Mexico has so many faces. The most bitter of them all is the poverty; the misery so many of our brothers and sisters drown in on a daily basis. And us? What do we do? We go to the theater on Sundays, after a grand family gathering culminating in a delicious, decadent feast. What happens to all those people who don't have water, electricity, food or medicine for their sicknesses? Just as my eyes have been blindfolded, a sector of our society is also blind. How many Mexicans are dying of hunger right now? And the rest of us, we just try to live our lives with as few complications as possible, thinking only about our own little problems...yes, we can criticize our political leaders' lack of responsibility, but we still don't see any further than our own noses. In Mexico when we see a woman who we so disrespectfully call a "María," (because she stands there with her shawl, with one of her four babies in her arms, and she begs), we all say "Handouts!" and look the other way, because we are seeing the poorest, most defenseless people in our country and we don't want to face it.

Handouts. So few of us know what it feels like to ask for money from strangers. It is an act in which misery trumps dignity. And there we all go, driving past them in our cars, looking at them from far away without the slightest twinge of emotion. The most we ever do is give them the smallest coin we have, and instantly we smile thinking about how wonderful we are for having done our one good deed for the day. How many children has that woman given birth to? Ten? Ten children who will grow up in the streets, where they will learn everything there is to know about life. There they will learn how to survive, and there they will learn how to die. Four of those ten children will enter a life of crime, for very early on they will learn the lesson that in the jungle only the strongest survive. And what about the little children who are left to fend for themselves on the streets? What kind of behavior can we expect from a fire-eater? They don't just burn their mouths and lips, they are burned on the inside and on the outside, and yet all we can see is something unpleasant; a blight on the landscape. And God help the windshield-washer who dares approach our new car; he might leave his filth all over it! "How irritating," we say. All that, just to earn a peso or two. But have any of us ever really thought about how hard it is for them to climb out of the hole, poorly dressed and poorly fed, with no motivation at all in life? Good God, what is all of this? These are the thoughts that accompany me as I fall asleep—that is, if I fall asleep at all, shedding tears and holding in so many more, grieving for what has become of Mexico, the country I love so dearly.

I always wake up earlier than my sister. This makes her very nervous, because the minute the men outside start hearing noises they come in to check up on us. I can tell she's annoyed at me. Not realizing it bothers her, I go to the bathroom and my flushing alerts Rudy who then knocks on the door and comes in, turning on the TV full blast. One day Laura asks me to please not get up—to just wait until the men come in on their own—not to flush the toilet. This, of course, makes things harder on me, and from that day on I wake up in the morning and just lie there, not moving. I look up at the ceiling and study it. As always, I see that one spotlight and the pastel-colored plaster moldings around it. My eyes travel over that hateful room with the open closet; the barred window with the white blinds which we are not allowed to go near, much less open; the door next to the spot on the floor where I sleep; and a small bureau next to my sister, decorated with her little card-sized images of Jesus, the

Virgin Mary, and St. Charbel, and a little lamp that we are only allowed to turn on at night. Those are the most unpleasant hours of the day, maybe because ever since I was a little girl, whenever the sun goes down, I always start to feel nostalgic, and the feeling always seems to grow and grow.... Whenever I hear the sound of the wheelbarrows coming around selling sweet potatoes, or a train whistle, I begin to feel a big hole open inside my chest; a hole that I can't seem to fill with anything.

FAITH

It is not in the stars to hold our destiny, but in ourselves.
—William Shakespeare

While held hostage, kidnapping victims often find strength in their religious faith, believing it will protect them and help them prevail over the forces of evil that have put their lives in jeopardy. I believe that God is our father and protector, and thanks to God and the power of my faith, I was able to emerge from this situation intact and alive. Part of my strength comes from always keeping the word "God" present in my mind:

> Graciously rescue me, God!
> Come quickly to help me, Lord!
> Confound and put to shame
> Those who seek my life.
> Turn back in disgrace
> Those who desire my ruin.
> Let those who say "Aha!"
> Turn back in their shame.

But may all who seek you
Rejoice and be glad in you.

—(*Psalm 70, Prayer for Divine Help*)

At some point we ask our captors to bring us candles and an image of Christ and the Virgin of Guadalupe. They bring us these images as well as a bit of holy water. How to make sense of this; that the murderer, the kidnapper, the criminal, even in the midst of committing his criminal acts, can believe in God as I do? On top of everything, they give us all that we ask for and more to fulfill our religious needs, so that we may find the spiritual sustenance we seek.

The darkness of that room has a way of crumpling the soul, and we feel beaten down by that complete and total solitude. We can barely tell the difference between day and night, and yet we wait to light our candle until we can sense that the sun has set. We begin to pray. Little by little our prayers lead us into a kind of trance, and I move my hands and body in rhythms that I have never before experienced. We do these things while still bombarded with all kinds of noise from the outside, with the television and the radio on, blasting out at two different frequencies and at full volume. Our spiritual volume, however, is somehow stronger than all those noises put together, and with the inexplicable power of prayer we carve out our own little corner of silence.

I have always thought of religion, or spiritual beliefs, as the supernatural guarantee that is offered to humans in the interest of their salvation. Religion comes from our desire to understand our existence, the incessant threats, anxieties, and fears that trouble our lives and foreshadow our death. We attribute secret, mysterious, unknowable causes to things like health and sickness, abundance and want, the good things we enjoy and the bad things that always seem to be lying in wait for us. Prayer allows us to understand that we have an awareness of the infinite. As the result of this experience, I come to understand that God exists.

Our captors are always asking us what we want, and on one particular day they are especially solicitous, bringing in candy and little cakes for us. Most surprisingly, however, they suddenly announce that they want to have a little party for us, to help ease the tension; the unpleasant atmosphere. They tell us we ought to try and relax a little, to get through this as calmly as possible.

"Tonight, then, we'll come in to see you. And don't worry; we're not going to do anything to you."

"Laura," I say to my sister once they've left the room, "What are we going to do? The idea of them coming in here and being with us terrifies me. What do they mean, a 'party?' That's the most ridiculous thing I've ever heard of. Maybe it's a trap…. Sure, now they're our friends, those human slime…."

"You know what?" Laura replied. "We're just going to put on the biggest sweatshirts we have in here. You pull your hair back, and we'll both make sure they can't see anything. OK?"

"All right."

As promised, they come to our room that night, and they find us sitting there waiting for them with our blindfolds already on, tied over the cotton balls pressed against our eyes—we had a big bag of cotton balls in our room to use for this purpose. They turn on a tape recorder so that we can listen to some music. They also bring peanuts, potato chips, and tequila. Pancho turns to us and says, "Look what we brought you: Tequila Cabrito…it's my favorite."

They pour us two little cups of tequila and offer us cigarettes, which we smoke with difficulty since we are blindfolded and have trouble locating our lips when we want to inhale.

As they joke around good-naturedly, they tell us not to worry, to relax a little. The Midget is not with them tonight, which calms me somewhat, and makes me feel more willing to cooperate. Again, they tell us everything is going to turn out all right, that there's no need to be afraid. The music and the banter escalate, getting friendlier and friendlier, as they continue to refill my cup with more and more tequila. I begin to feel the alcohol seeping into my body, giving me a tiny bit of freedom for the first time in this nightmare, and little by little I start to feel that I'm not afraid of anything; that I just want to laugh and have a good time.

They ask us about our lives and tell us about theirs. It's all a lot of fun, but nobody on either side of this dance dares to say anything too personal that could be compromising. The night wears on until finally Rudy can't take the smell of the cigarette smoke any more and he opens the window—a wonderful boon for me, since I am right next to it and the wind blows into the room like a wonderful gust sent in to clean that wretched cubicle of all the horrible smells, the pain, the confinement and now this drunken debauchery. That, in the end, is the real party: the air, my air, our air.

"The window is open," they say, "so don't make any noise. Outside they should only hear that we're in here together with the music on, that's all."

After a while they ask my sister to sing. She agrees, and in a low voice launches into *Paloma querida* and then another song I can't remember. Our kidnappers are impressed, and when she is finished, they applaud and tell her what a pretty voice she has; that she should sing professionally and make a record album. I just sit there, downing my tequila until I've forgotten what I'm doing there. Sometimes, I suppose, there are times when we need some kind of sedative to make reality a little less hellish.

If someone had filmed this scene of victims and kidnappers passing the time so cheerfully, the movie would have been nothing short of surreal—totally surreal. But there we are, all of us, just trying to have a good time.

After the party ends, they close the window and leave the bottle with us. Of course, they don't drink a thing that night because, as they tell us, they're working and they never drink on the job. In the end, I think they give us alcohol simply to get information out of us, which they don't, though they do achieve their purported goal of relaxing us. In that sense, at least, their party is most definitely a success.

After they leave, my sister and I take off our blindfolds and sit around drinking, listening to music and munching on peanuts and potato chips. At some point the two of us look at each other and we smile, both of us thinking how absurd all of this is.

"Titi, how did this happen to us? Oh, Titi, what is going to happen to us? Cheers! To our lives, and to our health! Let's drink to that!"

"Cheers!"

That night my sister and I cry, laugh, sing, smoke, get drunk and drag each other to the bathroom. We keep the party going, just the two of us, and though our laughter is silent, somehow we feel very contented that evening.

The next morning, when Rudy wakes us up to give us our breakfast, a nasty hangover is also there to greet us. My head is pounding and today the world seems very gray and small. After drinking a lot, I always feel vaguely guilty, depressed. How could I have laughed and had a good time with my kidnappers? And even worse, how could I have possibly felt happy? Buried under the blanket, my sister calls out good morning and asks me how I feel.

"Awful, my head hurts and I'm completely hung over."

"Oh, Titi, it smells awful; it's like there's a dead body somewhere in here. What could it be?"

"I don't know what you're talking about, I don't smell a thing."

"Titi, it's your breath! You're rotting away before my eyes!"

She is right. At this moment, I am rotting away before her eyes and mine. Because inside of me, right now, my faith is slowly dying.

When Rudy finally leaves, he sets our breakfast down on the floor, along with a few aspirin because all of them know that, like so many other victims before us, we finished off the bottle of tequila. Nothing new under the sun.

I rush into the bathroom to brush my teeth with soap, and then with a tiny bit of the toothpaste they gave us. Things seem to look up a little after that.

Laura and I have gotten into the habit of eating our food between the closet and the television set. First we take our coffee-colored blanket and we place it on the floor, and then we sit down in a lotus position with our food in front of us. Then my sister blesses the meal by rubbing her hands together and placing them over the food, and she asks God to be present here with us and to grant us health. Then she gives thanks that even during this horrible time at least we have food to eat. Sometimes she starts to cry, thinking about her children who aren't here to share the meal with us.

Even though we are in a filthy, non-descript room in an unknown location, we know that for our psychological health we must turn this place into our home. We have to take possession of the various spaces in the room so that we can feel there is some kind of order to things—an order that we have created.

The tiny corner of the room where we place the brown blanket becomes our dining room; that is where we always eat. Sometimes we pull the television stand over, but in general our dining area is that wedge of space between the closet and the television set. That is where we put everything, and we even venture to ask our caretakers for lemon and salt to season our meals. If we are still hungry, we sprinkle lemon and salt on the tortillas they give us, which turns those scraps of food into a tasty little dish.

When they are in a good mood, Pancho and Romeo bring us expensive food, from the Hunan restaurant, or else they treat us to classic Mexican sweets and sorbets. The frozen popsicle sticks they give us are delicious, but by the time they reach our hands they are always half-melted, and we know that they have been brought in from far away.

They aren't always generous, though. Sometimes Rudy complains that Romeo hasn't brought money for food and we have to settle for eggs and beans. But when there's money, boy is there food. Of course, we always end up paying for it in spades. Nothing from them ever comes free. Especially the kind, sympathetic attitude they occasionally adopt when they want to relax a little, since we all have so much time on our hands and they decide they need a break from all the pressure we are living under.

At some point, my sister stops talking. She just stops talking. When the men come in I always try to respond in a relatively pleasant tone, even when I feel awful. But one day, Laura simply decides not to speak to them at all. Several days go by like this, and it isn't just them—she stops speaking to me, too. And this makes me very nervous—nervous and scared.

"Laura," I tell her, "please don't stop speaking to me. I know you're in pain, that you're angry and hurt, but please don't stop talking to me because I'll go crazy if you do."

She stands there for a while, just looking at me. Then, finally, she breaks the silence, and says, "Titi, let's do some exercise." We hug. Both of us understand that in extreme situations like the one we're in, abrupt personality changes and mood swings just come with the territory. Rudy had given us a tattered, worn book that we could use to distract ourselves a bit. She begins to read to me from it, but I can't for the life of me figure out what she's talking about—a frog, or something, I don't know. Some of my memories are crystal-clear, while others are more vague, blurry, hard to piece together.

Sometimes we just sit there looking up at the ceiling for hours on end, waiting to fall asleep. We usually take a shower in the morning, after breakfast, and we watch TV, tuning in to a state-run channel with cultural programming. In the end, watching TV is always very unpleasant, because we have to keep the volume so high. Still, as time goes by we begin to filter out the TV noise and can actually hear the sounds of the night outside our room. When you hear that kind of blaring noise all day long, as incredible as it seems, eventually you don't even hear it at all anymore.

We ask to borrow the small, black radio so that we can listen to some classical music. If we turn on the radio we can turn off the television set, and so we are constantly asking them to lend it to us. Funny enough, whenever we use it for long periods of time, they inevitably want it back, and actually ask us to "lend" them "our" radio.

They allow us to turn off the TV at night, whenever we want. But we also know that turning off the TV means we have to go to bed and then we won't be able to make any noise at all, so we usually wait until we are really tired to turn it off.

It is terribly hard to fall asleep under these circumstances. The adrenaline never lets up, and sleeping in an unfamiliar house, always wondering when the door is going to suddenly fly open, hearing all sorts of noises, identifying the dogs by the sound of their paws, resting your head against a pillow that so many other hostages have laid their heads on, and smelling all the smells that have left their mark on that pillow...none of it is very pleasant, to say nothing of the mattress, which is practically torn to shreds from all the action it has seen—shreds of other people's feelings, maybe. According to them, of course, the mattress just came back from the dry cleaners. In general, I sleep with my head at my sister's feet. I like to sleep on my right side, so that I don't crush my heart, and I can never sleep with my back to the door—if they come in to kill me I don't want to get it from behind, I want them to look me in the face as they do it. My sister begs me to sleep closer to the door, because she is scared to death of what will happen if they came in. In a way, I guess she feels protected by my body.

That afternoon, my sister and I are praying when Romeo knocks at the door. We quickly throw the blanket over our heads so we won't see him.

"Hey, how are you doing? I came in to see you because I'm going to be gone for a few days. I have to go to Guadalajara to take care of some business. But I promise to bring back a delicious *pozole*, the best *pozole* in the world for you."

This ghost really likes to eat in style; he has already told us as much, and sometimes he even shares his food with us. One day he brings us char-grilled hamburgers, the most delicious I have ever tasted. Whenever he wants to spoil us he brings us food from wonderful restaurants, or dishes like spaghetti with *chile poblano* that, according to him, he makes himself.

"I'm worried about my family. Yesterday I went to see my mother and you know what? She had a little altar set up with a photo of you two that she cut out from some magazine."

"What do you mean from some magazine? People know that you've kidnapped us?" I ask.

"No, no...nothing like that. They mentioned it a couple of times in the papers, but it's all under wraps now because we didn't want the police to get wind of it. If that ever happens, the two of you are through."

Our captors are always careful to keep us in the dark about everything that happens on the outside. We know absolutely nothing of the Mexican public's overwhelming and very shocked response to our kidnapping.

"But, I don't understand. What happened with your mother?" I ask.

"She said to me, 'Oh, my goodness, those poor women! Can you imagine what those evil men are doing to them? How can people be so bad?' And I said to her, 'Enough, stop that nonsense.' But when I saw her eyes, how scared she was as she looked at me, I lowered my voice and said, 'No, Mother, I promise you those women are fine. Those people don't mistreat anyone; they're just doing a job. It's business to them, that's all.' And then she said to me, 'What do you mean they don't mistreat anyone? Can you imagine what it's like to be separated from your family, your children, trapped like that? Those kidnappers should be killed. I can't understand why they aren't all in prison for life. But anyway, I've prayed to the

Virgin of Guadalupe for them, and I'm lighting a candle for them to give them a little light in all that darkness.' And you know what? I felt so bad that I swore to myself, this is the last kidnapping for me…. And then there's my sister; she's about to get a divorce. I think my son-of-a-bitch of a brother-in-law is beating her. Poor bastard, because the minute I find out it's true, man, he doesn't know what he's got coming to him or who he's dealing with."

"But Romeo, really, why are you involved in this kind of thing?" I ask him. Today the ghost is very gregarious and I suddenly sense that it is very important for me to get as much information as I can out of him, and to listen. It is always so important to listen.

"I was young, very young when I left home. I've always been real independent and I don't like to have anyone paying my way—especially my mother who was widowed. So I decided to leave home and find a way to support my family. I went up north—a friend who lived on my street back home had gone up north, and he told me that when I wanted to become a real man, to give him a call. That's what I did, and that's how I ended up there. And that's also how I met the Lady of the Rings. She was the devil incarnate, but she had a kind of soft spot for me. I had no idea, but I was really skating on thin ice with that; I ended up working for one of the biggest drug trafficking organizations around. The Lady of the Rings was the only living survivor of her entire family. They had killed her father, her husband, all her brothers and almost all her children. The only ones left were her and one nine-year-old daughter. She was in charge of the northern branch of the cartel, and she was a murderer all right. 'I kill them before they can kill me.' That's what she always said. Every month she would send me to the U.S. to pick up and drop off stolen jewels, but she had this crazy fixation for rings. She was so crazy about rings that she always held onto the stones she liked the most and had rings made for them. She had all sorts of rings—big ones, little ones, thick ones, thin ones, some with rubies, or diamonds, made of gold, or silver. Anyway the point is, that old lady had so many rings—she had them from dead people, living people, and that was the only thing that made her happy in her life as the head honcho of this crime organization. Nobody dared to disagree with her. She had a huge ranch, just for her and her daughter. There were nine triggermen, and that's not counting the sharpshooters and the bodyguards that were always around her. They didn't leave her alone for one second, not even to go to the bathroom. They used me as a kind of companion, though she never let me hear a single one of her conversations. I realized what kind of business it was because when you spend so much time living with these people, you get to know things. She had that organization so well-controlled, everyone obeyed her orders down to the letter. And the drugs never touched her hands. She had everything running so perfectly that the drugs arrived direct from the car factory, and she had her men figure out how to put the goods inside the frame, the body, the dashboard—there are lots of ways to hide drugs in a new car. One day I went inside the house without being called in, and I heard her talk about how sick she was of a guy named Gutiérrez. She turned to three of her right-hand men and told them to bring him out to eat mud with the hogs. The next day I went out to see the hogs, to see what she meant by that and sure enough, I saw the most disgusting thing I ever laid eyes on: Gutiérrez's body cut up in chunks, and the hogs having a field day with the guy's head. That day I grabbed my things and went into hiding in the south of Mexico, scared to death that the Lady of the Rings would find me. Only after a few years did I go back to Mexico City; that was when I got into stealing cars. And then one day I ran into Pancho. We were friends when we were kids, and he told me I should get into these kidnappings. Let me tell you, it's a huge difference—this work is a hell of a lot more efficient, and not nearly as scary. It's the same risk, because if they catch us we know that we'll rot in jail. But if they catch me, man, I'd rather blow my own brains out than spend the rest of my life in jail. Anyway, I think I probably said too much...now you be good, and I'll see you in a few days."

After he leaves, my sister and I throw the blanket off and just sit there staring at each other, dumbfounded, completely incredulous, and we start praying again. So all these miserable criminals have their own stories of abuse, spiritual and physical. Is it possible that the pain is what turns them into such evil, spiteful people? Or is it the poverty? No…there are plenty of people who are poor but honest and well-meaning. I don't know what the answer is; only God knows why they are the way they are.

Another morning, Rudy comes in and turns on the television as loud as it will go. He doesn't offer even the slightest greeting, and I instantly know that something awful is about to come our way.

"Hi, Rudy," I call out. The only response I get is a loud kick to the door. He delivers us our breakfast, and says, "You aren't behaving. We don't want any noise, do you hear?"

"Yes, sir," I reply. I always try to be as respectful as possible with my captors. I think this is the wisest attitude to adopt, because at the very least it makes them marginally fond of me.

Two hours later they come in and take away the television, and the radio music playing outside the room is turned up so loud that the speakers seem ready to explode. We begin to panic; I am so nervous, I throw up. We hear loud footsteps, and lots of noise; we are petrified. Suddenly there's a knock and the men come into the room, and the Midget starts yelling, loud and furious. For me, his arrival is always like an explosion of fear; in addition to the fear I already feel, his presence makes it grow, for it permeates my entire being. I can feel it in every single part of my body.

"All right, you two, cover your eyes, RIGHT NOW! RIGHT NOW! This isn't a game, you stupid blondes. Your time has come, that is if you don't get to work and be good.... Now, one of you two has to leave. The talks are getting ugly and we have to let one of you go to take over the negotiations. This is your moment of truth. Let's see who's who here...who's going to *give up her life for the other one.*"

A deathly silence falls upon the room, and my heart starts to pound so loud and so fast that I think I may be having a heart attack. My sister is at my side, and both of us are blindfolded, and under the blanket. Our breath is the only sound I can hear in the room. The silence grows and grows, and so does my awareness that it will be me: I am going to be the one to give my life for my sister Laura.

"I'll stay," I answer.

"Are you sure?"

My sister says nothing. I can only feel her tears rolling down the bandages pressed tightly around our eyes and our souls.

"Yes, sir, I'm sure."

They remove the blanket covering us, and we are now sitting side by side on the bed, hugging our legs as if they were life itself. Suddenly, a hand begins to caress my head with incredible tenderness, and I hear a male voice that says, "That's the first time in this business I have ever seen that. In this bed we've seen fathers fight with sons, mothers fight with daughters, husbands and wives, brothers and sisters turning against each other. This sure came as a surprise. We didn't have to wait at all."

He continues stroking my head as he says this, and then suddenly he grabs my right hand, interlacing my fingers with his, and I am surprised to feel that his palm is damp with perspiration. He presses his hand over mine. I cannot describe the feelings that came over me right then: surprise, fear, anger, and frustration. Romeo then says to me, "Come on, we have to talk." Without letting go of my hand, he helps me up and leads me into the other room, the room where they sleep.

He places me on the bed face down, and he lies down next to me. The situation has now gone way beyond anything I could have ever imagined. I am suddenly so frightened that I am unable to utter a single word.

"Don't be afraid," he whispers in my ear as he begins to stroke my back gently. I move slightly, shrugging my shoulder to get him off me, to let him know that I do not want him to touch me. He removes his hand instantly, and apologizes.

"I want to know if you're sure that you want to stay instead of your sister."

"Yes," I reply.

"Why?"

"Because it's for the best." I get the feeling that Laura is nervous, very nervous, much more than me, and I know that she has begun to upset the captors with her reactions, her crying. And anyway, my sister didn't say anything when they asked us that question; clearly she was not prepared to give up her life for me, or maybe it was her survival instinct that kept her from saying anything. All I know is that this has been the hardest moment of my life, and the greatest test that God has ever placed in front of me. And if I had died I would still not regret that decision, because it is the greatest thing that I have ever shown to another human being. And when I say that, I mean to say that the person I have loved more than anyone else in the world is Laura Zapata, because she is the only person for whom I have ever offered my life.

When you ask yourself what life is all about, and then life presents this kind of situation, you suddenly understand that your existence has meaning. I was given the opportunity to love someone so much that I no longer mattered. The important thing was Laura. And that is what we are here to learn, to love one another—to love one another as if they were God. This, at least, is how I have come to see things, and this is the thinking that has led me to this moment—the greatest moment of my life.

In the other room, the Midget is grilling my sister about what she's going to do to get the money if they let her go. After many, many more questions they take me back into the room, and leave me and my sister alone for a moment or two.

"Titi?"

"Yes, Laura? I'm here."

"Forgive me. I'm a coward. Forgive me."

"Don't worry," I say, with a lump in my throat.

The men come back and the Midget asks us, "All right, Laura, now are you sure that if I let you go you're going to get the money I'm asking you for?"

"Yes, sir. Just yesterday, actually, I couldn't even sleep because I was thinking all night about what my family and I could do to get the money. I'm going to go to Joaquín López Doriga's news show and tell everyone that we're opening a bank account so that they can help us raise the money. I'll ask my friend the *"gordo"* Molina to help me with some television shows and I'll talk to Mr. Azcárraga, one of the owners of Televisa, and I'll ask all of them for help, sir, all of them."

"Well, you better, because we're holding on to your sister as insurance, and if you mess up, or if your family or your friends do…then her life isn't worth shit, you get it?"

"Yes, yes, sir."

While they continue talking, I feel as though I am hearing them through a dark, dark tunnel, and I know that at that moment they are pushing me into the darkest, most horrifying abyss that I never thought I would ever know in this life. I suddenly feel like an orphan, because I know that Laura is leaving and that she won't be with me anymore, and that my next steps are my most uncertain. And I can almost smell it; I can tell somehow that the worst is yet to come.

"…and maybe you'll never see her again, her children won't ever see her…."

"My daughters," I say. "My daughters…." And I begin to writhe in pain. My daughters. Right then Romeo takes hold of my hand and presses it hard.

"Don't worry," he says in a low voice. "You have to come with me now." He picks me up off the bed and I grab hold of my sister's hand with all the love and all the fear I feel. They separate us and Pancho, the one with the gruff voice, drags me, telling me to hang on to his back so that he can carry me down the stairs.

"Where are you taking me?" I ask, and Pancho just says,

"Shh...shh." I cling to his back, and as I make contact with him I can feel that he is a big, strong young man, and that his heart is pounding as uncontrollably as mine. How is it possible that these people willingly do all this and, inside this situation of their own doing, feel frightened or troubled? What makes them feel that way? The moment, the situation, us, the drugs, the fear? What is it? They take me to what seems like a tiny room downstairs, with a blaring television set.

"Now tell me, Ernestina, is Laura really the right one to go?" says the Midget, who is growing angrier by the minute. "Why not you? Don't make a mistake because if you do"—I can hear him kissing his fingers; I imagine him kissing a cross—"you're never going to see your daughters again."

Every time they say anything about my daughters, I suddenly regret my decision and want to tell them to let me go, that I'll do a better job negotiating. But at the same time I sense that if I let Laura stay she won't make it out alive.

"No, she's the one who should go," I say.

"You're really bugging the shit out of me, you know that? Who do you think you are, anyway? So, you're real calm and collected, huh, not afraid of me one bit, right? You know what I'm gonna do to you? I'm going to rip your clothes off and stick you in a water tank all naked, to see if you'll get scared of me then, how about that?"

At that, my legs buckle beneath me and once again, that familiar feeling, that hot surge of adrenaline takes over my body.

"No sir, I respect you. I fear you. It's just that I'm naturally calm. Please, I apologize."

"Bring me that AK-47," he calls out to one of his men. "I'm gonna give it to this goddamn bitch." The Midget is completely beside himself at this point. For some reason he is enraged by the decision that my sister should be the one to go.

I hear footsteps, the sound of people coming into and leaving the room, putting things on the wall, and then taking things down. I try to move but then, for the first time in my captivity, someone strikes me. I see stars and feel one side of my face go numb. Someone, with every last bit of strength, has just slammed me on the forehead with what felt like the butt of a gun. The blow is so powerful that I spin halfway around, swaying from one side to the other in an effort not to topple over. After that, they cover me with blankets and begin to hit me all over my body with objects that feel like clubs, weapons, and shoes. All I can do is just endure it, and my silent tears are immediately absorbed by the wads of cotton covering my eyes. Still, I somehow manage to remain quiet; not making any noise, for the real noise is inside my soul. Semi-conscious, or else numb from the pain, I can feel them pick me up and prop me up against the wall. There are no words to describe the feeling of being held at gunpoint, knowing that you are being beaten with a weapon that could go off at any moment.

"Oh, my God, don't let this be the moment of my death. I beg you Father, I beg you; please don't let this be the day of my death."

Suddenly I hear someone snap a photo. Now I understand. They want my family to see their Ernestina beaten, abused, and desperate.

DEATH

When we exist, death is not yet present, and
when death is present, then we do not exist.
—Epicurus

While I am kidnapped, the presence of death is always with me. Death is a natural fact. We all know it, but perhaps we don't bother fearing something that often feels so far away. We all have to die, but we don't really worry about death until death catches up with us. Only then do we begin to feel it. Then we suddenly feel overwhelmed by our vulnerability as humans, and it is never easy to assimilate, much less accept. During these endless hours of suffering, I say to myself, "Death is not an event that occurs in life; you can't live through death." Is it possible that death is a pure and simple fact, like birth? No, no—my parents taught me that death is the end of the life we know, but also the beginning of another kind of life-cycle. In other words, death is like the twilight of the sun that is, at the very same time, the same sun rising somewhere else. But then I think about how death separates the soul from the body, and I believe that my own soul, my spirit, is immortal. Death is a place of rest for us after all the counter-attacks our senses must endure, after all the restless motion that flings us from one place to another like puppets, after all the winding paths our rational minds take us down, and after all the care of looking after our bodies.

Death is the possibility of the impossibility of all existence. It is the potential absence of all the possibilities of man. I understand all of this, yet still, I DO NOT WANT TO DIE.

"Take the photo already. No, *pendejo*! No! Put the gun by her forehead. Don't let her move. Stay still, Ernestina. Did you hear me? I said stay still."

After a long while, I find myself lying on a cot, covered with blankets, tied up and blindfolded, sweating and crying. *Mamá, where are you, mama?*

Voices, footsteps, whistles, cars…they all come and go, until Rudy finally comes for me. He picks me up and leaves me in my bed. I think it's very early in the morning because I feel a chill; the chill of desperation and death. Lying down (after all the ghosts have finally left me alone), several hours go by before I can see again, because after being blindfolded for so long all you can see are shadows. As I remove the cotton I begin talking to my sister, but she is no longer there. I try to find her with my hands, with my voice, my will, but she is no longer a part of this story.

The next day when I wake up, my body, my soul, and my spirit ache. Alone, so alone, more alone than loneliness itself.... And now what? I don't get up. They leave me my food; I don't even bother to see what they've brought me. The first couple of days go by like that, more or less. On the third day, though, for no particular reason, my spirit lifts, giving me strength, and it tells me, "You are a child of God, and today you are alive. You have to hold on to your divine birthright, you cannot allow anyone or anything to defeat you." And with that, I get up and out of bed.

Rudy knocks at the door and comes in. "Good morning, Rudy. I'd like to take a shower. Can you turn the hot water on for me?"

"I'm so glad to see you're feeling better, ma'am, because this is going to take a lot longer than we thought."

Not even those words can make me falter. I take a long, long shower, rubbing my body—black-and-blue, beaten, but alive. Yes! My body is still alive. And the rest of me even more so. All right, you little men, today I proclaim my spirit is stronger than yours, and you will never get the best of me, never. In the name of God I say this and I will stand by this belief.

That afternoon I do a lot of exercise. A few days ago the men had given me exercise wheels to strengthen my back and stomach muscles, and today I put them to use. I sweat and sweat and sweat. Every droplet that comes out of my body is like a tiny bit of my anger, frustration and abandonment being released. But I also get to thinking:

"I am who I am, and I am here." Then I lie down and start watching television. They knock on the door and I quickly cover my head with the blanket. It's Romeo.

"Titi, forgive me for not being there to protect you from everything they did to you. Please forgive me! They wouldn't let me stay with you. They sent me out for the cars to bring your sister to the house where your family is staying. You know something? I'm starting to feel something very special for you, and that isn't good, because this is work and I'm not supposed to have any feelings for you."

He lies down behind me. I still have the blanket covering me but my back and my arms are bare. He takes my hand in his and begins to caress it. My first instinct is to wriggle free but he grabs my hand with such force that I can't move it at all.

"Calm down, Ernestina, stay calm," I tell myself, "He isn't going to do anything to you. No, no, no, he can't hurt me."

That night (like every night), my father Ernesto keeps me company. I always see him by the headboard of the bed, embracing me with his big arms. His death was a terrible blow to me, perhaps the worst in my life. And yet, in captivity, I can feel his presence and imagine him with a big smile, saying to me, "Everything's fine, and everything will be fine!"

Instead of telling me stories, my father liked to recite poems for me. There was one, by Rubén Darío, that he loved to read me—he read it so many times that I still know it by heart. Tonight, I fall asleep remembering those verses, and I am taken aback when I actually think about the words, because it almost seems as though my father

predicted that his little princess would one day live
through this tragedy:

The princess mourns—why is the Princess sighing?
Why from her lips are song and laughter dying?
Why does she droop upon her chair of gold?
Hushed is the music of her royal bower;
Beside her in a vase; a single flower
Swoons and forgets its petals to unfold.

The fool in scarlet pirouettes and flatters,
Within the hall the silly *dueña* chatters;
Without, the peacock's regal plumage gleams.
The Princess heeds them not; her thoughts are veering
Out through the gates of Dawn, past sight and hearing,
Where she pursues the phantoms of her dreams.

Is it a dream of China that lures her,
Or far Galconda's ruler who conjures her
But to unveil the laughter of her eyes?
He of the island realms of fragrant roses,
Whose treasure flashing diamond hoards discloses,
And pearls of Ormuz, rich beyond surmise?

Alas! The Princess longs to be a swallow,
To be a butterfly, to soar, to follow
The ray of light that climbs into the sun;
To greet the lilies, lost in Springtime wonder,

To ride upon the wind, to hear the thunder
Of ocean waves where monstrous billows run.

Her silver distaff fallen in disfavor,
Her magic globe shorn of its magic savor,
The swans that drift like snow across the lake,
The lotus in the garden pool—are mourning;
The dahlias and the jasmine flowers adorning
The palace gardens, sorrow for her sake.

Poor little captive of the blue-eyed glances!
A hundred Negroes with a hundred lances,
A hound, a sleepless dragon, guard her gates.
There in the marble of her palace prison
The little Princess of the roving vision,
Caught in her gold and gauzes, dreams and waits.

"Oh" (sighs the Princess), "Oh, to leave behind me
My marble cage, the golden chains that bind me,
The empty chrysalis the moth forsakes!
To fly to where a fairy Prince is dwelling—
O radiant vision past all mortal telling,
Brighter than April, or the day that breaks!"

"Hush, little Princess," whispers the good fairy,
"With sword and goshawk; on his charger airy,
The Prince draws near—the lover without blame.
Upon his wingéd steed the Prince is fleeting,

The conqueror of Death, to bring you greeting,
And with his kiss to touch your lips to flame!"[1]

The next day, in the morning, Rudy and Romeo come into my room.

"Get up, Sodi. We're going to take you out into the sun today."

"May I brush my teeth first?"

"All right, Sodi, get washed up. You can let your hair dry in the fresh air," says one of them.

"You can't complain, can you? It's your lucky day. The last time you saw or felt the sun was 24 days ago. You've got five minutes."

"Both of you know I have no way of telling the time, but I'll hurry up."

They close the door, and an inexplicable fear surges through my veins. Are they telling me the truth? Or are they going to move me somewhere else, or rape me? For God's sake, Ernestina, calm down, calm down, I tell myself. They only want to take you outside. Yesterday one of those miserable men said that you looked pretty beat-up, and asked you if you were feeling all right. God, oh God, don't leave me now!

I am standing there holding the cotton balls over my eyes, waiting for them to come in and tie the blindfold around my head. I feel so sorry for myself, completely frightened by these brutish men, following their orders

---

[1] "Sonatina" by Rubén Darío, translated by John Pierrepont Rice and published in Hispanic Anthology: Poems translated from the Spanish by English and North American Poets. Ed. Thomas Walsh. New York: G.P. Putnam's Sons, 1920.

and fulfilling their wishes like a little doll, sitting at the edge of the bed with my legs pressed together, my eyes covered and my hands intertwined, waiting for the arrival of God only knows who to come around and treat me like an animal to be taken to some godforsaken place, who knows where.

They knock on the door and Rudy comes inside to tie the blindfold over the cotton balls.

"All right, Sodi. Get up now."

Taking me by the forearm he guides me over to the door and we go past the room where they sleep, where Romeo placed me face down on the bed and touched my back. As we walk down the little corridor I begin to hear very loud music. It seems that they've taken me to some kind of balcony that, after a few minutes, I realize is quite big. Rudy sits me down on the balcony floor and orders me to take my sweatshirt off. Thank God I have a small black, tight-fitting lycra shirt on underneath. It is the one item I still have from the clothes I was wearing the night we were kidnapped, and I always wear it. Every night I wash it and, incredibly, it dries in a matter of hours in that squalid little cubicle. I still have it, in fact, and whenever I feel sad or depressed I put it on to remind myself that life is life and it is the only one I have. Whenever I feel the need to protect myself during some time of crisis, I put it on, to remind myself that I am a survivor, and that fear is not part of my philosophy of life. I have learned how to control it and it does not stop me from acting or being.

Sitting on the floor, little by little I begin to feel the heat that caresses my face thanks to the presence of "*el gordo*," (the big guy) as I like to call the sun, and the light and heat slowly travel down to my arms. I try to hike my pants up above my knees in an effort to nourish my entire body with that blessed light.

Not satisfied with just feeling the sun, my pores open wide to receive all the air around me, and with that, my happiness is absolute and complete. I breathe with such energy, trying to hold on to that fresh air in my body for all eternity. After a few seconds, though, something yanks me out of my reverie, and I come crashing to the ground in an instant. It's the Midget's voice, hovering just over my right shoulder, asking me if I like it. Another voice to my left asks me if I want water. Another voice, in front of me, tells me that I'm very white, and asks me if I want to hike up my pants. One by one I begin to hear each of the voices that make up this team of kidnappers, some seven or eight men who chat among themselves, watching me, like a little monkey sitting on the floor with a terrified face, whirling my head around in every direction trying to figure out the source of each of the voices calling out.

"Titi...why do they call you Titi?"

"Because instead of Tina, my father called me Titi."

"All right, Titi, tell us about yourself. You have two daughters, don't you? What are they like?"

Whenever they touch on the subject of my daughters, I never answer them. As time goes by they eventually realize that they cannot speak to me about them. I sigh heavily. My mind flutters as I ask myself the question, "What is breath?" Breath is uniquely individual, from the first breath we take to our last exhalation; it is ours and only ours. The time of your death is when the body ceases to breathe, saying goodbye to life with the sound of an exhalation. Our breath is our link to this marvelous and terrible condition of the body. All of the feelings that are considered "higher"—melancholy, nostalgia, the absence of God—are all connected to the body, in one way or another. What we call angst (or the pain of the soul), exists in the body, for in this material world of ours, the soul expresses itself through the body. For example, when I am separated from the man I love, I feel that separation like I would the amputation of an arm, an eye, a leg. It is the kind of pain that turns into a kind of material energy, but we exist as spirits, his and mine, and we love each other beyond form, time, and space, and our love is so great that, in the end, we cannot and need not suffer.

"What's the matter, you don't want to answer us?"

"Yes, oh—I'm sorry. I was a little distracted, that's all."

They start talking and eating, and they offer me some fruit which they bring to my mouth. This day is absolutely marvelous, and the sun fills me with a tremendous desire to live, helping me gather strength for whatever comes my way.

Rudy comes into the room every morning to clean, and he always brings me food or cigarettes, which he metes out parsimoniously—some days I get two, other days I get four. When he isn't stoned, he usually starts talking. More than once he offers me marijuana, and I always tell him no, please don't offer me any of that garbage. Rudy explains to me that it will help take the edge off things—the kidnapping, the captivity. This makes me angry and I refuse to answer him when he says that.

"You know something, Ernestina? The group wants to get you together with the other guy we kidnapped, in the other house we've got."

"What for?"

"Well, it would be cool, don't you think? His father's an important businessman —but he's not young, or anything. He's got to be around forty-six years old, this guy, and he's always drunk. He's real expensive for us, too. We have to buy him cigarettes and a bottle of whisky every day, and the day after, he always ends up asking for aspirin and an antacid for the stomach pain. Anyway, yesterday we all laughed a lot thinking about what the two of you'd do together. They want to bring him in here to sleep with you. Who knows—maybe with you he'd sober up a little. The poor guy just babbles on and on, nobody understands a thing he says. What do you think?"

"I think you're all sick."

"Oh, don't get mad. The guy before you two, he was one scary dude. He was always yelling at us, and once he said, 'You're all just a bunch of cowards, you're all chicken shits. The only way you can beat me is when you're all together, ganging up on me.' Then he challenged each of us to a fight, one on one. And so we said sure, and one by one we all fought him. We all saw how he hit the first guy, and then we went, one after the other, and that monster, man, he beat the shit out of us, and we couldn't let him do that. And so all of us, pissed off and with our noses bleeding all over the place, we decided to take control of this guy. But he punched in the walls and said that if he didn't sleep nobody else was going to sleep either, and man, he wasn't afraid of anyone. If we put a pistol to his head he just put it in his mouth and said, 'Come on, faggot, kill me. Just let me see your face when you do it, I don't want to miss out on looking my murderer in the eye. You're such cowards that you can't look a man in the eye when you kill him.'

"Then the boss came by. When he saw us, he got so mad he decided to hang the guy. He gave us orders to tie his hands and feet, and to hang him from the ceiling with a noose around his neck. When we lifted him up to hang him, he started to move around like a little puppet and his face got all red. Finally, after all that, the boss decided to let him loose, and he said to the guy, 'Next time you die, you shit.' And when the men finally untied him he still managed to curse at them. 'Fucking faggots,' he said. 'The only reason you all do this is so that you can be together, as men.' Whenever I think about that I still get pissed off. And you know what? That motherfucker got off safe and sound because he was one of the best-paid jobs we ever pulled off. But back to what I was talking about—you want to meet the guy we kidnapped?"

Instead of answering him I decide to ask him a question. I already know that my salvation will always be art.

"Have you ever heard of Oscar Wilde?"

"No, what's that?"

"He's a wonderful man, from England. A great writer and poet. I'm going to tell you a story. It's called *The Nightingale and the Rose*." And I tell him the sad story of the nightingale who sees a lovelorn student yearning to find a beautiful red rose for his beloved, and how the nightingale helps him find the rose, but dies in the undertaking. The student, of course, never knows what the nightingale did for him.

"When the rose does not achieve the result the student hoped for, he tosses the rose into the street where the carriages and horses trample it, trampling over the nightingale's sacrifice...." I finish the story.

"Ernestina, do you forgive me for everything?" Rudy suddenly asks me. "I swear this is my last kidnapping."

I know this is a lie, but I also know that there is no heart that does not soften in the presence of art.

"Rudy, if you will stop offering me drugs, I will give you a present."

"Come on, Sodi, what can you give me?"

"I'm going to give you a diamond ring."

"Come on, what do you mean, a diamond ring?"

"I'm not going to tell you anything else. Go into the bathroom and take the bottle of shampoo. Inside you'll find a beautiful ring. And I promise not to tell anyone about it. OK?"

"Thanks, Sodi. Thanks for everything. I really love your stories. When I get bored sometime you can tell me another one."

"All right, Rudy."

One afternoon Romeo appears. I am sitting on the floor listening to the radio, staring off at nothing in particular when he raps on the door. Immediately, I cover my head with a green and brown striped towel. They finally washed it for me, because for the past few days every time I put it on it stank from the constant dampness and it had begun to sprout fungus. I stopped using it and began to use the blanket instead, but with the blanket on they couldn't hear me very well and, of course, they couldn't see me, either. I would cover myself entirely and sit down, hugging my legs, my head between my knees. All they could see was a big lump under the blanket, and they got sick of it—plus, they wanted to see something of me; even just my feet, my arms, my hair. One day, finally, they asked me for the towel and washed it.

"Hello, Titi! My little Titi! I love how you wait for me. Look what I brought you."

"You know perfectly well I can't see, and I don't 'wait' for you. Do I need to remind you that I have been kidnapped and can't leave?" I reply.

"Forgive me, I'm so stupid. Hold out your arms."

Very tenderly he takes hold of my arms, extending them and turning them so that my palms are facing up. At first I think he is going to hit me in my palms, but then suddenly I feel something quite heavy that forces me to bend my arms, and then I notice the scent, which is so strong that for a minute I can't think…the only thing that exists right then is my sense of smell. Yes! Yes! I smell roses, fresh roses. Real roses.

"Do you like them? I bought them, with all the love I feel for you."

"What?"

"Yes, Ernestina. I love you very deeply."

Sitting in that tiny, dark room with a towel over my head, kidnapped, with more than five dozen roses in my arms, I now have a kidnapper telling me he is in love with me?

"My God, you've got to be kidding! This is insane."

"No, my love. It's not a joke. I love you."

"Listen, Romeo, I am not your 'love' or anything else. You and your friends have kidnapped me, and that is an act of hatred, of pain. You cannot talk to me about love. So please, leave me alone, just go."

"I understand, I understand…calm down. I don't know what's happening to me, and I'm going to pay for it but I can't help it."

Standing behind me now, he places his hand under the towel, searching for something. Tilting my head back slightly, he lifts the towel from behind and he strokes my hair until his hand brushes the nape of my neck. Breathing heavily he moves in closer, his lips grazing my skin. Finally he gives me a tiny kiss on the nape of my neck; a kiss filled with all sorts of feelings that I do not share. In the middle of this, I manage to catch a glimpse of his hand and I see a tiny scar just below his thumb.

"I'm sorry, I'm sorry." He stands up, leaving me with a towel on my head, more than five dozen roses in my arms, and feeling so out of control that I wonder if I might go crazy.

When Romeo leaves, I get up with the flowers in my arms and I set them down on the bed. Only when I remove the towel do I finally see them; they are big and beautiful. How can it be that in the middle of all that horror, God has sent me these lovely roses to give me a bit of joy, color, fragrance? Is this a divine message telling me to hold onto hope? I hug them and begin to cry because these flowers are so exquisite, and I cry for all the flowers I have received in my lifetime; flowers that I never bothered to touch or smell; flowers that gave their lives up for me, for love, for Mother's Day, from boyfriends, for birthdays. To think of all the precious flowers I have been given and never once noticed. But these flowers in partic-ular have come from far away to tell me something about life—yes, my life. Thank you, God. But what can I think of this person who gave them to me? Oh, God. Have mercy on me.

Suddenly there is another knock at the door, and I put the towel back over my head. As always I stay in bed and Rudy comes in.

"Wow, wow, look what we have here. We have a real life Romeo in the house, don't we? I wonder what the boss is going to say about this. You've been a bad girl, haven't you?"

"No. I haven't done anything. He's the one who's doing this. I am a decent woman and I don't like any of this."

"Yeah, sure," he says, kicking the door as he leaves the room.

From then on, all the men start to call him Romeo. To avoid confusion, I have called him Romeo from the beginning. But the nickname really begins to be used here.

STOCKHOLM SYNDROME

I don't fear hell for its pain, but because
it is a place where love does not exist.
—Saint Teresa

In 1973, a group of robbers went into a bank in Stockholm, Sweden, took four hostages, and held them for six days. When the hostages were freed, they refused to testify against their kidnappers, and even paid for the defense of their kidnappers out of their own pockets. One hostage fell in love with her captor. According to other versions of this story, the woman was seen on camera kissing one of the criminals. Psychologists dubbed this type of seemingly odd behavior the "Stockholm Syndrome."

When people are kidnapped and spend a prolonged and indefinite period of time with nobody other than their captors, they sometimes develop feelings of affection for them.

Psychological studies have shown that the Stockholm Syndrome is an emotional response that affects hostages as the result of the feelings of extreme vulnerability and defenselessness produced by captivity. This striking episode in Stockholm prompted a wave of psychological studies describing the emotional bond that sometimes emerges between hostage and captor after several days together.

Psychologists define this syndrome as a relationship of emotional dependence that evolves between a victim and an aggressor when the aggressor deliberately threatens the life of the victim, but does not follow through on the threat. The victims will generally try and keep the aggressor happy, and this strategy often becomes an obsession, as the victim begins to show feelings of gratitude and affection for the person who is, in fact, doing them a great deal of harm. Victims often feel such overwhelming relief when the aggressor withdraws the death threat, that they may suddenly feel intensely positive feelings for the aggressor which, combined as they are with fear, make it very difficult for victims to hate their aggressor. For these reasons, it is not unusual for some victims to consider the aggressors to be good people.

The case of Kristin (one of the hostages taken in the Stockholm bank robbery), is an interesting example of what happens to some women under these circumstances. Kristin was unable to speak, eat, or go to the bathroom without the permission of her captor, an armed criminal. According to one specialist, Kristin was "not only terrorized but she was infantilized as well. Children cannot survive without the care and nutrition provided by their parents, and they do not know the meaning of the word 'love.'" The specialist goes on to explain that babies and small children experience relief when their hunger is sated, when the wet diaper is replaced with a dry one, when they are given clean sheets. "We might call these experiences of infancy and childhood 'precursors' to love; a profound gratitude for the gift of life, expressed through feelings of contentedness. Often, contentedness is a response to the feeling of being relieved of unpleasantness and pain. Kristin denied that the source of her pain was Olafson, one of her captors. Many hostages deny, suppress, or forget that fact. When this happens, the victims are only able to see a person who has chosen not to kill them, despite having had the power to do so, and instead gives them food and permission to speak and go to the bathroom. The victims often feel very grateful for this."

Many years must go by before these bonds are finally broken and the victims truly realize and accept what has happened to them. "Many people who have been taken hostage have expressed these same feelings...they state that they do not want to feel love or compassion for a murderer (many hostages have seen their captors kill other hostages), and that they have even struggled to not feel affection," one specialist notes. But very often they establish a closeness with one of their captors, often the one who feeds them. "If the age and sex happen to be right, the victims can certainly end up feeling something akin to romantic love." Kristin, the hostage in Sweden, became Olafson's lover, and broke off her engagement to another man because of this.

In my case, I tend to think that the Stockholm Syndrome, if it existed at all, occurred in reverse. Romeo felt a great deal of love and affection for me, and ultimately that is what saved my life.

One night, Romeo knocks at the door and comes in my room with a bottle of Martell cognac, soda, ice and two glasses. He also brings potato chips and peanuts.

"Hello, my darling. You're going to have to put your blindfold on, because I want to talk to you and I don't want you to see me."

I put the cotton over my eyes, and he ties the blindfold around my head, undoing my ponytail holder and freeing my hair. Then he sits me down against the wall, and turns on some Luis Miguel music on a little tape player he has brought in with him.

"*Usted es la culpable de todas mis angustias, de todos mis quebrantos....*" (*You are to blame for all my pain, for all my heartbreak....*)

He immediately fills the glasses with cognac and adds the ice and the soda. I can't see anything, of course, but I can hear him fixing the drinks. At first I am afraid he is going to slip some kind of drug in the drink, and I don't want to take the tiniest sip of what he gives me, but I don't have a choice because he raises the glass to my lips and presses it against my mouth.

"You're going to like it—it's called Paris at Night, just like this wonderful night. Don't be afraid, I won't do anything you don't want me to do. You want to know something? My real name is Daniel Dante. Are you surprised? Well, now I am in your hands and you can do whatever you want with me. My sign is Cancer, and they say we love to spend time at home."

While he's saying all this, he lights a cigarette and gives it to me to smoke, and then he lights one for himself. Since I can't see, I try to stick it in my mouth but my aim is sometimes off and he helps me smoke it.

"I'm twenty-six years old," he tells me. "And I'm in the carwash business. Now, with the kidnappings and all, things are going pretty well for me and I'm expanding my business. We steal cars too, and we use the carwashes to change the license plates and repaint the cars, and we get them out in less than a week. I'm about to open up some shops to sell mirrors, car horns, wax to clean the upholstery, all sorts of things for cars; just about anything you can think of. And you know what? With the money I made off the last kidnapping I just bought a piece of property, so I can build some condominiums—I still don't know whether I'll rent them out or sell them though."

As his monologue enters my brain I gulp down the wonderful drink that allows me to forget, even if for just a moment, the hell that I am in. Because everything he says deeply disgusts me. Hearing about all the possessions he has and doesn't deserve, possessions that have been paid for by the suffering of his victims and their families, enrages me.

"Would you pour me a little more Paris by Night?"

"Of course, my darling, whatever you say."

He lies down on the floor and gently pulls me down with him, resting my head on his stomach. He says nothing for a long while, just stroking my hair as we listen to Luis Miguel. What do I feel? Well, right now I feel that life is totally insane, that none of us have any idea what we are doing here (least of all me), as I lie here trying to survive, my head resting on the belly of one of the men who has kidnapped me.

After a while he gets up and pulls me along with him, propping me up against the wall again. Then he asks me a question.

"May I kiss you?"

"Of course not," I reply.

"All right, all right, I won't do anything you don't want to do. I have a Camaro. Have you ever seen one?"

"No. I don't know anything about cars."

"It's the most incredible car. You wouldn't believe my neighbors, though; they've got a lot of nerve—one is sixteen, the other's eighteen and they're always asking me to borrow my Mercedes Benz. They're really starting to piss me off but I have to act normal around them so they don't catch on about the kidnappings. Can you imagine? They don't know anything about me. My neighbors, they all say that I'm like a role model to everyone because I pay for my nephews' tuition."

"Right, with the money and suffering of other human beings."

"Oh, don't be like that.... Oh, I'm sorry. I'm so rude; forgive me. Let me pour you another drink, and here's another cigarette.... Darling, listen, there's something I've been wanting to tell you. When you decided to stay here so that your sister could leave, that day I got goose bumps because every other kidnapping was so different—everyone always fought to be the first one to go...and that was the moment I started to have feelings for you. I never thought that you were the strong one, because your sister was really the one who seemed that way. But things turned out the way they did and, well, life is full of surprises, I guess."

Suddenly he stops talking and I feel his lips press against mine.

Taking my head in his hands, he kisses me with such passion that a spontaneous feeling of revulsion courses through my body and I don't know what to say or do. This is the last thing I expect, and to make things worse, when you are unable to see, all your other senses are sharpened. It is such an unbelievably filthy feeling that I cannot even begin to describe it.

"Romeo, or Dante, or whatever your name is, will you please leave me alone, please?"

"All right, beautiful, I'll leave but I want you to know that I am in love with you. Good night." He moves closer to me and kisses me again, slipping his tongue inside my mouth with the confidence of someone who knows exactly what he's doing.

Today, and on many other days, he sings me a song by the Mexican singer Ricardo Arjona:

El problema no es hallarte
El problema es olvidarte
El problema no es tu ausencia
El problema es que espero
El problema no es problema
El problema es que me duele....

[The problem is not finding you
The problem is forgetting you
The problem is not your absence
The problem is that I wait for you
The problem is not the problem
The problem is that it hurts....]

Later that day the Midget shows up at the house, and barks at me. "You have to talk to your fucking sister. Everything she told us is bullshit. You have to make her understand that we are going to kill you and if she doesn't do what she said she'd do, you're never going to see your daughters again. Ernestina, this isn't a game. We've already lost a lot of time and money for your family to pull a fast one on us now."

Already blindfolded, they tie up my hands and feet, take me out and shove me into the trunk of a Chevrolet-type sedan. The first thing I feel is the total absence of air, and it is hideous. Then, when they cover me with the blanket I really start to panic. It is the most terrifying feeling I have ever experienced. In the darkness of the trunk, I am positive they aren't taking me to speak with my sister, that they're bringing me to some empty lot where they're going to kill me and dump my body in a sewer.

Inside that trunk, without air, sweating and feeling the close hand of death, all I have left is prayer. Oh, how I understand all those other people who have been victims of crime, but who haven't had the good fortune that I have had. I understand them because I have lived through everything they have, only I have been spared the culminating moment of murder. Everything I experience that night is the same macabre vigil that so many others before me have had to endure.

After about an hour we finally arrive somewhere, though I have no idea where. The car stops and my heart races, impelled by the fear of death inside me; as always, superseding any other emotions that I might be able to feel. They open the trunk and the gust of air that blows over me is blessed and glorious. All I care about at this instant is air; that wonderful air that enters my lungs and my spirit.

They sit me down, still inside the trunk, and take the blanket off me. Still blindfolded and bound, they place a cell phone next to my ear and order me to talk.

"Laura, how much money do you have?"

"Oh, my darling Titi, we have…. But things aren't what we thought. Please, Titi, don't cry. That money in dollars is going to be impossible!"

"Laura, Laura! Sell my property, sell my house, please! Oh, my God, help me, help me!"

"I already spoke to the people about your property and they can't sell anything without your signature. This kind of thing can't be done overnight."

"Talk, talk...talk to Licenciada Nava. Please, oh please, help me!"

"Titi, stay calm; trust us. Trust me, Titi, I am begging you."

"If anything happens to me I will blame you for it; you and the rest of the family. Tell my daughters that if they end up without a mother, it was your fault!"

The men hang up the phone and place me back in the trunk, covering me once again with the blanket. Alone, so alone, I begin to cry.

On the way back I realize that my chances for survival are running out. Because my sister could have easily told a very different story; she could have said, "Titi, don't worry, it's all going well, we're going to get you out of there," but none of that has happened. All she told me was that things were going badly. I know her, and when she doesn't tell me that things are moving along, all my hope of being freed crumbles.

When we return to the house, everyone is furious. The Midget shoves me, hard, into a corner of the room.

"You see, you fucking *pendeja*, I told you your family was going to let you die. They don't love you. They haven't gotten the money together, so you see? They don't give a shit about you. I ought to just kill you now." With that, he pulls out his gun and presses it against my temple. Suddenly I am overcome by the most powerful adrenaline surge I have ever felt in my entire life. It is a force that enters my body through the soles of my feet, and climbs up to the top of my head where, suddenly, without even thinking, my ability to reason simply snaps. With my right hand I grab the barrel of the gun and begin to pound it against my own temple, screaming at them, "Look at me, you idiot, look at me. You can kill me now! Yes, now! And don't threaten me anymore! I'm sick and tired of you people. You're all pathetic, always together all the time so that you can feel powerful, when you're really just a bunch of faggots, so kill me already and leave me in peace! Do it already, please! Kill me!"

I scream and I cry. That is exactly what I want right then: death.

We all experience times of sadness and pain over the course of our lives, but there is one thing that is especially hard, perhaps the most difficult truth to assimilate: death. The number of relatives and friends we've lost over the years, and the way we've lived through those times will determine, to some extent, how we will confront our own death. People who have managed to never think about death either out of lack of experience, or simple avoidance or omission, may have managed to avoid the bad feelings, but they will likely be far more vulnerable to any circumstance that puts them directly in front of this fact.

As an inevitable reality, death can be confronted in several ways: through faith, outright denial, through resignation, or acceptance. When our lives are peaceful, we don't have any real immediate need to consider the question of death, but it is an idea that becomes more and more present inside of us as we grow older. There are two particularly ambiguous aspects that can exacerbate the anxiety many of us feel about death: first, the idea that it may happen at any given moment and we will be unable to do anything to prevent it—for example, that we could be suddenly killed by an accident or a heart attack. The second thing that is so troubling is the question of what happens afterwards—if our existence ends with death, or if we transcend to another reality; a paradise, perhaps. When these uncertainties start to weigh on us, we may take measures of extreme precaution to try and ensure that death does not catch us by surprise—constant medical checkups, traveling as little as possible.... But to be able to confront the reality of death and break free from the cycle of tough questions and vague answers, we must evaluate the possibility that our fears are plausible, and not the product of obsessions or fixations. We have to face that possibility of our own death—though it may be unlikely—and move ahead nonetheless. We have to live life knowing that it may be taken from us at any moment. There is no point in letting fear rule our lives, because fear can often end up becoming its own insidious form of captivity. The problem is, thinking about it makes us feel very bad. And feeling bad is no fun, but it's almost unavoidable that thinking about such a complicated topic wouldn't lead to obsessive thoughts running through our heads over and over. In other words, it is impossible to be absolutely certain of something so impossible to control. Seen in that light, we may be able to reach a level of acceptance that, while slightly irritating, is far more bearable than fixating on the excruciating uncertainty surrounding the concept of death.

I cannot bear it any more. I have been constantly thinking about when this time would come, and now it is here, right in front of me; a pistol pressed against my head. They want me to explain why my family hasn't come up with the money. But I can't take it any more, and so if this is my time to go, then so be it....

Suddenly I hear Pancho's voice.

"Wow, this lady sure has balls."

After that, there is silence. All the men leave the room, and I stay where I am, crying, trembling. I start to vomit, and once again I ask myself, *Mamá, where are you?*

The next day, nobody bothers me at all; no food, no water, no noise. That night I drink water from the toilet because I have nothing else to drink and I am dying of thirst. I can live without food but not without water. And so with the little cup where I normally keep a candle, I drink that water. And I think, "Oh, Ernestina, once upon a time you were married in a castle in the outskirts of Paris, with all the luxuries and beautiful things that life had given you. Now, here you are drinking toilet water to survive. But it doesn't matter. What matters is that you are alive...." That whole night, all I can think of is my mother. I wonder what she is feeling right now. Is she with my sisters? I speak to her silently:

"Mother, here I am, where the past and the present meet. Mother, I want to give you thanks, because your womb was the first universe I ever knew, and it was not cold; your womb possessed the most amazing colors and flavors. And only I can tell you what was there inside of you, because I lived there and grew there. That is how I know how your heart sounds on rainy afternoons. I know how your blood runs when the sun comes out. You have never tasted your blood, but I have, and I know how your body tastes from the inside. Those things made me, shaped me and held me tight. Maybe it is never enough, but today, the day I might die, today, mother, today is forever. So today, mother, near or far, wherever you are, I know you are suffering for your children, and today, mother, I want to thank you for loving me, for giving me life, for existing. Today, Mamá, life is cruel and it has spattered us with the spiritual mutilations of eternity. Today, on the brink of death, I feel the moment has come to tell you that I have been happy; for God, for you, for my daughters. Mother, I pray for your blessing for whatever destiny awaits me...."

And then I fell asleep, exhausted.

The next day is the same as the day before; no food, no noise, just the black fear of eternity.

One more day and Rudy makes his appearance, just as before.

"Good morning. I've brought you breakfast."

"Thank you, Rudy." He gives me cereal and fruit,

which I devour like a starved animal. I can feel him looking at me like one of those people who go hunting for food in garbage cans, because if you are hungry enough you will do anything; things that would be unthinkable in any other circumstance.

After a lot of thought, I decide that God has put me through all this to make me consciously aware of the suffering of others; to unite me with them and their experience. What I have actually learned is the meaning of compassion; understanding it as a kind of participation in the suffering of others. Compassion, for me, is the very essence of love between living things.

That night, all the men go out partying. The Midget, apparently, had pledged to the Virgin of Guadalupe that he would not drink for three years. And tonight, those three years are up. Why would he stop drinking like that? Who knows, but it is just my luck that the damned Midget decides to go and get drunk tonight.

I go to bed early, around ten in the evening. Besides me, the only one in the house is Rudy. In my dreams I hear noises, and I wake up; it must be around four in the morning. First I hear laughter, then I hear someone kicking things around; a lot of noise. Terror invades the room and my heart, when suddenly I hear a knock on the door. I cover my head with the blanket, and the door opens.

"Titi, can I come in?" It's Romeo, drunk. "Titi, I want to make love to you."

I am paralyzed, unable to respond. He approaches me and gives me the towel to cover my face so that I can remove the blanket. Right away I sit up. All I can say is, "Get out. Get out of the room."

Romeo grabs me by the neck, pulling me close to his mouth, and says, "Tonight you're going to be mine. You got that?"

My sobs come out in the most incredible way. Suddenly they are just there, defending my integrity, screaming NO with all the energy I have. No, don't do that to me! Please don't do that to me!

"Romeo, please don't do this to me. I don't want to have sex with you. That would be rape. I don't want anything with you. I already have enough to think about without you starting in with this."

"You listen to me," he said, yanking my hair violently. "All the guys are hot for you, so now, you decide—you either do it with everyone, or just with me. If I make you mine, nobody else can go after you because we have rules about that kind of thing here, and one of them is that nobody messes with another guy's girl. You decide."

Immediately my survival instinct tells me that I am going to have to give in. No way am I going to endure a gang rape. I need to calm down first, though, to think about what I can possibly do to get out of something that may be inevitable.

I fall to my knees on the bed, cling to him, crying, and say, "All right Romeo, I am only going to ask you for one favor. Please use a condom because I am very afraid of getting AIDS. For the love of God, don't hurt me! I have never done anything to harm you. I thought all you wanted was our money—why this? This is evil, please, don't do it."

"A condom? I don't have any condoms here. All right, fine, but get ready for me tomorrow, because tomorrow I'm going to make you mine. Anyway, I'm exhausted tonight. So it's set, my love. Tomorrow will be our honeymoon."

He comes closer and kisses my closed lips. His saliva tastes salty.

The next day Romeo comes into the room, primped and preened for a poor butterfly that has already lost her wings. That butterfly of course is me, with my mortal fear, trembling before someone else's will, trying to survive in this spiritual cesspool.

"Sweetheart, I want to make you happy today, because you have given me back my life."

He comes closer. His breath smells minty and he has put on an aftershave lotion that I will never forget. But the odor of that body is a tattoo that I carry with me in my nasal passages. If I were to smell him again, I would recognize him in an instant. He approaches me silently, like an animal waiting to pounce. He approaches me silently, with ardor, pain, force, with, with, with….

First he covers my eyes, pulling my hair out of the blindfold, tied over the wads of cotton. I don't know why, but Romeo has a fixation with my hair. Every time he touches it he pulls out a little comb and begins to comb it; this must calm him in some way. But what insanity; this mental patient acts as if he's playing with a Barbie doll. Not only is he disturbed, but he is incredibly infantile. And he goes on combing my hair as if he had all the time in the world. And me…well, my time is up. When he is done combing my hair, he lays back down on the bed and says, "My love, I want to make you the most womanly woman in the world today. You're going to be so happy today, because that's my responsibility. I swear it. You are going to fall in love with me."

When he says that, I can't help feeling as if I am losing my sanity again. How can this man think that I could possibly feel anything for him in any way at all? Doesn't he understand that he is raping me?

I am a lump at the disposal of…I don't even know who. This man is every man; he has no face, he could be anyone at all; what do I know? *Oh God, is this what you want for me?*

He begins to remove my clothes, kissing me everywhere. And I lie there thinking about my dignity, about my femininity that has been robbed by a ghost. Romeo stands up and begins to lick my fingers slowly; I can feel his tongue going from one finger to the other. An evil, lingering tongue, filled with his venomous saliva. He slowly climbs up my body with a serenity that only he feels.

"Darling, I am going to make you so happy...."

"Romeo, if the others come in, are they all going to rape me?"

I begin to cry as I imagine the Midget coming in, beating Romeo up, and then raping me. And the others coming in after they're through.

"No, honey, no. They won't hurt you. They know you're mine now. I already told them that I'm taking care of you. The boss warned me, he said I hope you're not making a mistake. He understands me, though, and he knows I'm in love with you."

And so he continues living out his fantasy inside my nightmare. He caresses me like no other man has ever caressed me before. In his insanity, this psychopath sees me as some kind of white goddess, and I can tell he feels a strong need to treat me as delicately as possible. I suppose that he never imagined he would ever have a woman like me in his arms.

"You're so white, so beautiful. Do you like that?"

First he kidnapped me, now he rapes me. How can this imbecile think that I could feel pleasure? For me, this is an atrocity, an attack against me, compounded by the fear that other people will enter the room, watch us, and want to join in this demented, depraved scene. Oh, God! This is insanity. He kisses me for what seems like hours, touching me everywhere and feeling perfectly wonderful as I lie there wanting to die, thinking "Why, God? Why?"

The ghost places the condom in my hand and says, "I want you to know, and I mean this, that I don't want to hurt you in any way. Put it on me, that way you can be totally sure."

"Hurt me? Don't you realize how much you're hurting me?"

"Shh, shh...everything's fine, come, come, my love...."

And that is how evil, theft, death, captivity, humiliation, all in the body of one man, enter my being. The possession goes on and on and on. But I will never give him the pleasure of possessing my soul; he only succeeds in taking ownership of my body for a short while, never my true being. And that is a lot, because I have somehow managed to hold on to the most precious part of me.

What kind of marks from him still remain with me?

Every kind.

When he is through he curls up next to me. I can feel his sweat.

"You know something, my love? The other night when we went out, the boss started drinking again and we went to a table dance and it was full of all these gorgeous Cuban women. We were at a bar in the Zona Rosa. Anyway, one of those dancers came up to me; she wanted me. And the boss called over four of these gorgeous women to drink with us, and one of them sits down on my lap, but I pushed her away because I couldn't think about anyone but you. We had a real good time, too, but before we left there was a raid and we all got held inside the club. And all of us, man, were we ever sweating, because, I mean, think about it—it's one thing to be caught with cocaine, but it's a whole different thing to be caught for kidnapping. They took our money, but at least we got out of there all right."

"Romeo, do you do drugs?"

"No, darling. They do but I don't—they do drugs, and a lot of them, too. What about you?"

"No, I hate drugs. I'm afraid of them."

"Can I stay with you?"

"No. Go." In general I try to be friendly and respectful with my captors, to avoid problems. But today, under the circumstances, I just can't.

"All right, I'll go, and I'm going to leave the condom on the bed so that you know I played straight with you."

When Romeo leaves, I take off my blindfold and see the condom, filled with semen, dangling from the headboard. I march straight over to the toilet and flush it down, and then I go into the tub to take a bath with cold water because at this house I can't ask the men to turn the boiler on. With that blessed water I remove all the shame and humiliation I have had to endure on this heinous journey.

Since they always go through the garbage, I have nowhere to put the condom wrapper. I don't want anyone to find out that I have been raped, and so I place it inside a Coke can, and I stick in a little piece of paper on top of it to make sure that nobody realizes what has happened to me.

The next day, I wake up, eat breakfast, watch television and do a bit of exercise. Suddenly someone knocks on the door and I cover myself. It's the Midget.

"Hi. I want to talk to you."

"Yes, sir. What is it?"

"Listen," he says, dragging me out of my corner and sitting me down on the floor. My heart is beating so fast that I am afraid it might stop altogether. I lie there face up, the towel over my head.

He lies down next to me and starts breathing heavily, very heavily, into my ear. I can feel the little hairs on my skin move back and forth with his exhalations and inhalations. But it isn't just him; the heavier he breathes, the heavier I breathe, in a bizarre escalation of emotional intensity, until finally neither of us can control it any longer, and the two of us begin to pant like beasts, one lying next to the other. My breathing is, as far as I can tell, brought on by the sheer terror I feel. But him? What is he so upset about?

"Have you behaved yourself?" he says, his breathing still labored.

"Yes, sir."

"I want you to tell me if one of my boys has mistreated you in any way."

"No, sir, none of them." My heart and my instinct tell me that I cannot tell the Midget that one of his men has raped me.

"Are you sure, now? You can't lie to me; you know that, because if I find out that you've been lying to me I'll kill you. You got that?"

My mind is spinning and I feel completely out of control, but I have to pull myself together so that he believes me.

"You know, you're very pretty. And I want to tell you that if you and I make love today I won't cut off your finger. Because the big guys upstairs already gave me orders to cut off your finger so that your fucking family will finally pay up. But if you want, we can cut a deal between you and me."

He lifts the towel so that it hovers just above my mouth and he moves closer—so close that I lose control of my bowels and I defecate. Thanks to this little stroke of Mother Nature, the Midget's libido turns cold, but his anger lingers on for several days.

He leaves the room and I get up, crushed. Once again I get into the tub to take a bath. My body is covered with the excrement of this senseless reality. The bath water is ice-cold, and with what little soap I have left, I practically scrub off a layer of skin; but there is no way to scrub off the emptiness that invades my body and soul.

MAGICAL THINKING

Good things happen to people with
a sweet and happy character.
—Voltaire

When held in captivity, people often experience the phenomenon known as magical thinking.

When I was a little girl, I used to lie down to rest in a spot close to the window so that I could feel the sun on my face. There were many flies in this spot. As I watched them for hours on end, I thought about how if I ate a little piece of bread I could become very, very small and then fly out of a tiny little opening in the window and out into the garden. In my vision, the flies became my friends, and invited me to their party. They were cheerful, always laughing, and hard-working, too. They carried me through a tunnel to a beautiful sunflower. When I arrived at the top, the petals were wide-open and resplendent, waiting for all the flies. The sunflower's yellow petals were dazzlingly bright. At the top of the flower there were little blue tables with chairs, and we all began to dance to the music of the sun. All around there were tiny little straws so that we could sip the sunflower's nectar. Everything was lovely and magical in that place.

In captivity, I imagine that I eat that little piece of magic bread and become very, very small. Then I grow wings so I can fly. But my problem is that everything is locked up; I have no way out. The window is closed and covered with bars. How can I get out of here? It occurs to me that I can try to escape through the crack under the door, a tiny sliver of space I can squeeze through, if I crouch down and flatten my wings. I am a little worried that one of my kidnappers might not see me and could step on me, but once I am outside this room, I tell myself, I will look for a window or an open space where I can fly far, far away from this place. As I think about this, the hours of my captivity fly, just as I wish I could.

That morning Romeo comes in and plants a big kiss on my forehead.

"You know what, my darling? Last night I had dinner with the boss and he told me that you really love me. He told me that he asked you if any of us had touched you and you said no. He said you did that to protect me. And that made me so happy...."

With goose bumps, I ask him, "Did you tell him about what you did to me?"

"Of course. We can't go around lying to each other."

"Oh, my God! Romeo, what is all this?"

"Life, Titi. It's life."

Is this life? I suppose. It is destiny; that inevitable

force imposed on each and every one of us. I am like an animal led to the slaughter, as destiny would have it. But what I want to know is what do you want from me now, goddamned destiny? Do you want to leave me with no fingers? Do you want them to kill me like a rat? Would you have them rob me of another piece of my dignity, every day? Is that what you want for me, destiny? A destiny I once loved, is that what you want? Who are you? What are you? Are you so great that you decide the day of my death, and my loves, my successes? Maybe you are the mind of God. I don't know.

The days to follow are the most bitter and terrifying of all.

The Midget barges into my room again, like the spoiled-brat son-of-the-devil himself. This man revolts me; he smells like hatred. He is revulsion incarnate. I experience something so indescribably grotesque whenever I sense his presence; just smelling him provokes feelings of danger, pain, and pure loathing. All I want to do is protect myself and flee. And yet, I cannot express the fear, the panic, the terror this creature inspires in me. Today, I am deathly afraid that the one thing I don't want to happen is going to happen to me.

"Ernestina, get up. I told you already, if your fucking family doesn't do what they're supposed to do, we're going to have to hurt you. They've given us no choice; we have to cut your finger off."

"No! Please sir, please don't cut my finger. Please...." I start to cry. I feel I am losing my mind. My finger, my body. How can they mutilate me? Are they human beings? Or are they monsters?

He blindfolds me, pushes me to the wall and gets me to sit down with a blow to the head. I begin to feel the symptoms of another panic attack. I lose control and begin to shiver uncontrollably. My jaw and my teeth chatter. In this moment I feel that I finally understand what they write about in horror stories. My hands and legs react with involuntary movements and the chill that runs through my body is the sensation of death itself. Maybe I am not going to die right now, not all of me at least, but I can feel my body responding to the possibility that one little part of it might die. My finger!

"Please, sir, cut one of my toes, but not one of my fingers."

"Enough talking. I can't cut off your toe because then you'd lose your balance, and anyway a finger is what will give your family the shock they need. I can't even believe I'm answering you! You deserve this for having such a shitty fucking family. Can you picture your finger in a box of cereal, and how your family is going to go crazy looking for it?"

As he says this, he grabs my left hand. Three or four other people join him, all of them silent; only their breathing alerts me to their presence. All of us in that room stink of adrenaline and inhumanity. They take my hand and they all have to help hold it down, because it is trembling so violently. As I cry out, one of them places a towel over my mouth, and I can feel them pricking my finger with a needle. I can't even feel the pain, and I can tell that he, too, is frightened. They all remain silent until one of them says, "All right, let's wait until it goes numb."

They leave the room and I begin to feel a chill in my pinky finger, and little by little it grows colder and colder until it is finally icy numb.

Suddenly I hear screams, people arguing, and I think I hear Romeo's voice in the middle of it all. Then I hear the sound of guns being cocked, insults flying back and forth, and several thuds against the wall. As all this is happening, I feel suspended; nothing can change my state of mind. The noises and the thuds continue for about twenty minutes, and I slowly begin to feel the effects of the anesthesia wear off. First it is a kind of tingly feeling, and then I can once again move my finger, which is mine and not mine. My body also stops trembling.

Someone comes into the room and my stomach cramps, but this time it's Romeo.

"My Titi, my Titi. They're not going to cut off your finger. I got so mad that I threatened to leave the group if they did that to you. The boss and I went head to head for the first time ever. He got tough, but I was even tougher. He found out what I'm made of today and you know what? I don't even care. We made a deal. The money that I'm supposed to get from the kidnapping goes to him, and that's it. I couldn't let them do that to you."

"Romeo, thank you, thank you." I embrace him, crying and kissing his hands like a little girl. I kiss them until my tears and my lips dry up. The impact and the stress of everything that has happened today is so powerful that I simply fall asleep right there—I don't know when, or how, but I just fall asleep. As if someone had hit me hard in the head, knocking me out and I cannot remember a thing. I have no idea what happened after that. All I know is that when the morning comes I am lying down on the floor, with the bedspread over my body. I take the blindfold off, and I still can't see. But what do I care about seeing is if my hands, which I touch and touch, are intact? I drag myself over to the bed, climb into it and rest my defeated, exhausted body. At some point that day I tell myself, "It's over and done, and like everything else that has already happened, it's dead because it won't come back. It's over, it's all over."

NEGOTIATIONS

While all this is happening to me, my family is living through their own kind of hell. My family records their conversations with the kidnappers, and what follows is an exact transcription of the kidnappers' negotiations with my sister Laura.

Phone call #1:

"Hello?" says Laura.

"Why do you give me that shit, why do you do that? Don't start with that bullshit."

"I did what you asked me to. I'm waiting for answers from the people who will lend us the money."

"Your fucking sister, ever since you left, she refuses to eat. She's getting desperate now, things are starting to get bad...."

The kidnappers hang up.

Phone call #2:

"Yes?"

"How much money do you have? You're playing fucking games. We're going to do what we said to you; we're going to have to start beating her up."

"No, sir, please, we're...."

The kidnappers hang up.

Phone call #3:

"We've got instructions to end this bullshit already," one of the kidnappers says. "You're not doing your part and the amount you're offering is a joke. We've got orders to cut your sister's fingers off. She already said we could cut off her little toe, but we're not even going to ask her this time; we're going to cut off her fingers."

"Oh, please don't say that, give us a chance...."

"Shut up. We let you go because we thought you'd be good for something outside, but you've been dicking us around."

"No, sir, really, look...."

"Shut up. We're going to kill your sister. And we don't care what happens."

"Listen, we have all the reporters on top of us, we can't leave the house...."

The kidnappers hang up.

Phone call #4

"Hello?" says Laura.

"Right now, one of the men upstairs is going to see your sister, and I can't be responsible for what he does to her. They're going to beat the shit out of her, and I don't know what else. If you don't hold up your end of the deal, neither do we. I want you to go to the news and ask people to help you."

"But sir, we can't leave here. The press and the police are outside...."

The kidnappers hang up.

Phone call #5

"Yes?"

"How are things going?"

"Good, I'm working...."

"How are things going?"

"We have gotten the money up to...."

"You haven't gotten anywhere. You're playing games, and you have to understand that your sister isn't going to be as lucky as you were. She gave her life for you and you're sending her to the slaughterhouse. What a piece of shit you are. I'm not talking to you anymore. These guys want to end this already."

"I need a chance. We're trying hard to put all the money together, just like you asked. Please don't hurt my sister...."

"Your sister already realizes she isn't going to make it out of this; she already asked us to shoot her in the head."

"No, sir, please...!"

The kidnappers hang up.

Phone call #6

"Tell me how much you've got now," says one of the kidnappers.

"We have.... That's what we've got."

"Are you an idiot or what? That's nothing. We want...."

"Sir, that kind of money is not realistic. My sister's funds in the United States have been frozen, and she is putting together everything she has here in Mexico. Please...."

"Tell your fucking pretty little sister the beauty queen that even if she has bodyguards we're still going to scare the shit out of her, and with you it'll be worse because we trusted you. What have you done?"

"No, please, no! No!"

"Don't fuck with me; I know you're fucking with me. Fucking money.... Motherfucking whore, we're gonna fuck you over, you goddamn bitch."

"No, sir, please don't say that...."

"For the rest of your life you're going to regret hanging on to a few extra pesos...."

"Don't say that!"

"What do you want, bitch? You cheap fucking whore, what do you want? Didn't you say you'd get it when you were here with us, didn't you? Now that you're out you get all cocky, right, you fucking whore, because you're not the one dying, right? You miserable bitch, you're not scared because they aren't your goddamn fingers and it isn't your goddamn life. I'm gonna tell you something, you disgusting whore, if you don't turn up with the money by Friday, I'm not taking any more risks with my men. So listen up. If you don't get the money, I'm not talking to you anymore."

"Sir, we are getting the money, but that amount is impossible. Nobody has that kind of money in cash. Please...."

"You already pissed me off, you cheap whore. I don't want to hear any more."

The kidnapper hangs up.

Phone call #7

"Why don't you pick up faster? Answer faster, bitch!"

"Yes, sir."

"Did you get the finger or what?"

"No, sir, please, not that!"

"Listen up now; tomorrow I'm going to send you the other finger, and if you don't find it, or if they don't want to send it to you that's not my problem. Shut up and stop crying already. If you keep on crying I'm going to hang up and I'm going to kick the crap out of your sister, so that she's mutilated and beat up. Get it?"

"Yes, sir."

"As far as I'm concerned you're a whore and none of the guys in here would have ever looked at you. When are you going to have our money?"

"Listen, sir, if I had it now I would give it to you."

"Shut up and listen. I am going to call you in twenty days, but tomorrow I'm going to send you another finger so you'll find it this time."

"You do not have to do that to my sister! Please...."

The kidnappers hang up.

Phone call #8

"You know I'm serious about the finger and about beating the shit out of your sister...and then, it's all over. Tomorrow, I'm going to call you to tell you because I know you didn't get the finger I sent you."

"No!"

"Today I took my time, and I'm not sending my men for fucking garbage! If you want your sister and your brother-in-law to keep their money, everyone real happy and all, we can just send you your sister full of gunshots; we'll just dump her in a ditch. And you'll see who wins. I'm the one who can give the order to kill your sister and fuck her over whenever I want. And every time your sister gets the shit kicked out of her it's your fault. We already did it to her once. They kicked her everywhere, even under her teeth!"

The kidnappers hang up.

Phone call #9

"How much have you got?"

"We've got...."

"You fucking bag lady. Did anyone hit you?"

"No, sir."

"Did anyone rape you?"

"No, sir."

"Well ever since you decided not to cooperate

things have changed and let me tell you, you didn't see anything compared to what your sister's been through. All the torture you're putting your sister through, man, that's exactly the same shit that you would have gotten but you got out thanks to her. You got out and you aren't even grateful enough to help her. You're an evil woman. We aren't beggars and I'm not going to send my men out for that kind of bullshit money, and expose them, expose myself. Keep your money. And I want to tell you that I swore off drinking, but today that's going to end. Tonight is my first night drinking after four years on the wagon. And if you come looking for me, I'll come to the house and then I'll tell you straight out...listen Laura, since your sister wasn't worth shit to you I'm going to shoot her in the head so that you can hear it, so that you can say 'that guy, he really had balls.' And I'm going to tell you, 'listen, I want you to hear me kill your sister.'"

"Please, sir...."

"Don't beg. Just tell me when you've got the money."

The kidnapper hangs up.

Phone call #10

"You're listening, right? Tonight your sister got the shit beat out of her for the second time. Unfortunately for you, I've been drinking, and I don't give a shit about any of this anymore, and I feel like going out and killing someone and let me tell you, your sister's the perfect person to do it to. And when I tell you she's dead, she's dead. Tomorrow I'm sending you another finger, because you didn't want to come out for the other one."

"We looked for it but we didn't find it."

"Shut up. Tomorrow you're going to look for the other one, and then, when you have your sister's finger, we'll talk. I don't know what's going on but tomorrow, if you don't tell me which goddamn finger I sent you, we're gonna have it out, you and me. All right?"

"Yes, sir."

"And tell your pretty little sister there, that the problem wasn't with the blonde, the problem is with her and her fucking husband. You got out because of Titi, and now she's the one who's suffering the most of anyone."

"God have mercy."

"Shut up and don't talk to me about God. The girl knows what it's like to lose a finger, and one finger is nothing, but two, well…. And if you piss me off I'm going to cut off all her fingers so that when you perform in your next play she won't be able to clap for you…. Even though you get so much applause, don't you? All right, I'm tired. I want my money. I know you've got the police there with you."

"No, sir. The whole family is putting in what they can. We don't want my sister to get hurt."

"Shut up. I'll kill her before I let the police get to us, and if they get us the second bullet is going to be mine, because what the hell is the point of life if you have to live it in jail like a rat? So, you go and tell those people advising you that they run along so that I don't kill her. Get it?"

"Sir, I promise you we are completely alone!"

The kidnappers hang up.

Phone call #11

"How much have you got?"

"We have…."

"Remember how I told you we've got people upstairs?"

"Yes, sir."

"Well, listen. All I want to know is how much money you've got, that's all."

"We've got…."

"I was a stupid shit for letting you go. Who freed you?"

"You did, sir."

"I'm going to make your life a living hell. Did you get the finger or not?"

"Oh, please!"

"Tell me. Did you get it? We left it where we said we would; stuck under that phone booth with a letter your sister wrote before we cut it off. Did you pick it up or not? Tell me, do you have it or don't you?"

"No."

"All right then, I'm going to send you another one. The people you've got with you are a bunch of assholes; they can't even find a fucking finger."

"No, sir, I don't have anyone with me."

"We should have kept you here. I bet your sister would have done a better job than you. So, let me tell you where things stand: your sister's stump is already infected."

And the phone call I make to my sister, after the kidnappers drove with me in the trunk of the car:

"Laura, how much money do you have?"

"Oh, my darling Titi, we have…. But things aren't what we thought. Please, Titi, don't cry, that money in dollars is going to be impossible!"

"Laura, Laura, sell my property, sell my house, please! Oh, my God, help me, help me!"

"I already spoke to the people about your property and they can't sell anything without your signature. This kind of thing can't be done overnight."

"Talk, talk…talk to Licenciada Nava. Please, oh please, help me!"

"Titi, stay calm; trust us. Trust me, Titi, I am begging you."

"If anything happens to me I will blame you for it; you and the rest of the family. Tell my daughters that if they end up without a mother, it was your fault!"

The kidnappers hang up.

There are 34 phone calls in all.

I soon find out that the U.S. bank accounts of my sister and her husband have been frozen immediately, because my brother-in-law alerted the U.S. government about the kidnapping so that they might send some specialists to handle the case. Naturally, he did this because he thought it the best way to solve the situation. Unfortunately, however, this created a chaotic mess, because it seems that people in the U.S. don't quite understand the nature of the kidnapping machine in Mexico. In the United States, blackmail is illegal. It is considered a crime to participate on either side of a blackmail in the negotiation of a kidnapping. This, however, doesn't mean that the authorities can't offer support and get involved in the negotiation process. At first, my case was handled by a private negotiator, who had some problems dealing with the American agents. That was when my sister Federica went to the AFI, following the advice of Licenciado Omar Saavedra, secretary of the Mexican president's wife, Martha Sahagún de Fox. I am deeply grateful to both of them for their kindness.

This was how and why my sister gathered everything she had in Mexico and ultimately paid the ransom.

Another day goes by. What day is it? I have no idea; it is just another day. But at night...I could never have imagined what Romeo has in store for me tonight; one more night in captivity. A serenade.

The first thing I hear is the sound of mariachis outside the safe-house. Romeo yells up to me, "I love you, baby, I love you!"

From his voice, I can tell he's been drinking. As his blood alcohol level rises higher and higher, he dedicates various songs to me. The ones I can remember are "*Señora bonita,*" "*Tus ojos,*" "*Amor de mis amores,*" and "*Somos novios,*" among others. This is like a scene out of a twisted horror movie; never in my wildest dreams could I have pictured this. How can a mariachi band possibly be out there playing songs for a kidnapper, dedicated to his victim? Is Romeo insane? Now I am even more terrified than before because this lunatic is obviously completely deranged. I don't know which is worse: the fear that he is evil or the fear that he is insane. I doubt those mariachis have any idea that they are participating in a spectacle engineered by a psychopath "in love" with his victim. Nevertheless, I can't help saying to myself, "Thank you, God, for letting this happen, because this is what saved my fingers and maybe even my life."

The serenade goes on and on, until Romeo finally comes knocking on my door.

"Titi, can I come in?"

"No."

"Titi, I'm coming in. Did you like your serenade? It was nice, wasn't it?"

Romeo comes in, talking on and on. Locking myself up in the bathroom, I don't answer him. When he realizes this he begins to tap on the door, and then he says, "Listen, I wrote you a poem. I brought you my own serenade. Open the door!"
My silence bothers him.

"I saved your finger...come on, open the door. It's the least I deserve."

When he sees that I am not going to respond, he slips a piece of paper under the door. Right now I am breaking a major rule—I am never allowed to lock myself in the bathroom, not even to take a shower. This makes him very angry, and he bangs on the door repeatedly.

"All right, all right, but tomorrow I'm coming in for you no matter what," he calls out.

When I hear the door close outside I pick the paper off the floor. It says:

I belong to the night.
You belong to the day.
I have a gang.
You have a family.
I always wait.
You always live.
I am a realist.
You are a dreamer.
I work with weapons.
You work with poetry.
I am a man.
You are a woman.
I cry for you.
And so do you.
With love, Romeo.

That night I cry for my daughters. I miss them so terribly, and I wonder how they are handling all of this. Who is looking after them? I think of them, my beautiful and cherished daughters, and I say, "If I never hold you in my arms again, I won't feel guilty. I won't, because I have hugged you and kissed you until my heart was filled to overflowing with your scent, your smiles, your everything. When you were born, I saw how you came into the world. And I didn't want any anesthesia, not even a little, because I wanted to experience your births as fully as I could. The pain was the least of it. The most important thing was the fact that a new life was emerging from my body, a piece of flesh—of my flesh—that from one moment to the next, would separate itself from me to become an independent being. That was how you were born, and what I saw was the very greatest thing I have ever laid eyes on. As soon as birth separated us, you were living and breathing in the air of this planet for the first time. The umbilical cord still united us, and you were my daughters…and those were the most beautiful colors I have ever seen…colors I could never have imagined; the red of our lives, joined by a green and an intense shade of blue, as intense as the miracle that the universe was witnessing.

"I remember how, on both those days, the doctor set you down in the same place: my chest. And he asked me, 'Are you happy?'"

I answered, "If there are five or six people anywhere on this earth who are truly, truly happy right now, then I am one of them."

"I want to tell you, my daughters, that everything in this life was worth it for the simple fact that you exist, and that God gave me the opportunity to know you and to love you. You have been the reason for everything in my life; because of you I have been the person who has worked to give you everything I am, have been, and will be.

"Camila, I love you.

"Marina, I love you.

"And if I have to leave you with something, my daughters, I leave you the great love I feel for you; I leave you the ethics that I have helped instill in you; I leave you respect for your fellow humans, and the knowledge that you owe nothing to anyone—not even your smiles. I leave you the culture and the art that are the greatest and most powerful weapons you can use to fight for things in this world. I leave you the sisterly love you feel for each other. I leave you as examples the joy of living and simplicity. And finally, my daughters, I leave you the truth; the truth that will never allow you to be slaves to anyone, not even yourselves. I love you, I love you, I love you." These thoughts bring me serenity. My daughters, though they are far away, bring me serenity.

The next morning, I wash my black shirt and I try to read a book, but I read without reading. My mind and my subconscious keep me on high alert at all times. I begin to discover incredible things about my body. Whenever one of my captors comes near me, the fine hairs on my arm stand on end. I push them down, to try and get them to lie flat, but they are rebellious and remain standing, prepared for whatever may come, just like me. Oddly enough, they always seem to rise up and lean slightly in the direction of the door where my captors come in. I can be on the right or the left side of the room, in the bed or on the floor, and those hairs always move in the direction of the door. Only when the men leave the room do the hairs lay back down at rest, but if they remain standing at attention it is because the men are coming back, and those hairs never once get it wrong. I come to see how our body hair protects us from our environment, but they also serve as our antennae. Just like a cat's hair stands on end when the cat gets angry or scared, my body hair does the same.

My body reacts to the kidnapping in other ways, as well. My menstruation stops. My period should have come during my first few days in captivity, but it never does. I guess my body very wisely stops that particular biological function as a way of protecting me from a situation that is unfamiliar and dangerous.

Water and wind appear over and over again in my dreams, and more than once I dream of a cave that devours me with giant teeth. As this happens, I can feel water running and wind that whips me in the face so hard that I can barely breathe.

In the end, I come to see my experience as a kind of madness; a dark reality designed by people who see themselves as gods. These men are paranoid, schizophrenic, always thinking that they are being pursued, that people are listening to their conversations. I note a deep sense of mistrust among them, and this makes sense because they are all aware that they are committing a crime, and they know that if the authorities catch them, they are ruined. Drunk with power, they want to be the gods that either spare or sacrifice the life of one of their fellow men, depending on their whim. This makes them feel omnipotent, and this feeling is reinforced by the financial benefits they reap. Nevertheless, I feel that they also live with a great deal of fear, though it is very different from the kind of fear that plagues me.

Their wives, girlfriends, and mothers are afraid of them; their children obey them without a word, and as for their victims…we beg them, we cry, we plead with them not to take our lives. These criminals can never change because their minds and their world-view are warped. I don't know whether it is society itself that turns them into monsters, or if they are born this way, but one thing remains crystal-clear to me: they are very sick people.

At one point, some of them tell me that they don't even care about the money anymore. The reason they keep doing this is that they can't live without the adrenaline rush that comes from doing something so dangerous. And they tell me that when they aren't involved in a kidnapping they go out and bungee jump, or go skydiving, just so they can feel a little of the high that they have gotten addicted to. They tell me that sometimes they drive out to an open road, where they dare each other to drive at speeds over 100 miles an hour. And I think they take drugs for the same reason—for that adrenaline fix, to help mask all of the anxiety and tension inside of them.

That afternoon, the Midget comes into the room and starts asking me a lot of questions.

"What kind of jewelry have you got?"

"I have four diamond rings, two gold bracelets, a sapphire ring, necklace and earrings, pearl necklaces and a lot of other things I can't think of right now. They're in a safe deposit box. My oldest daughter knows where they are."

"Listen, with the shit your family's offering us, that jewelry might just be what's going to save your ass."

I have no idea what is happening on the outside. I don't understand why the negotiations aren't moving forward. I get very nervous at the thought that they are rooting around like stray dogs for whatever we have. Then they ask me about the cars I own, and they tell me they want the deed to my house—or else I'll have to sell it to raise more money. I tell them that there is a mortgage for my house, which is a lie, but what else can I do? I have to keep a roof over my daughters' heads. And I know that if I agree to sell my house, I will have to spend even more time in this miserable hellhole, with the time it would take to carry out a transaction like that. I think about my jewelry and I begin to cry, because that, it seems, is what the value of my life has come down to: a bunch of stupid jewelry. Right then, I look up toward the sky and I swear to God that if I ever get out of this place alive, I will never wear another piece of jewelry as long as I live. That will serve as a reminder to myself of how deluded we all are, losing sight of the truth and the essence of our selves. Never, never will I let anything material become more important than me.

When I tell them that I have four diamond rings, I think about how each of those rings represents someone who I have loved dearly. Behind each ring is a wonderful, meaningful love story. When I got divorced, I decided I would not remarry—first and foremost for my daughters. I just felt that it would be unfair to force a stepfather on them. I don't believe in mixing things up like that— stepfathers, stepmothers, stepchildren. I wanted my daughters to grow up peacefully, in an atmosphere of love, freedom, respect, and art, not exposing them to unnecessary complications. This doesn't mean that I gave up love. I have always had someone at my side. I have loved deeply, and I have been loved deeply in return. But it was always the same thing, whenever the time came; the marriage proposal and the engagement ring in hand. I always refused. In all my relationships, eventually I found myself between the proverbial rock and the hard place: either we get married or it's over. And my answer was always the same: it's over. Each time, I tried to return the engagement rings, but they all refused to take them back. So that is why I have a little treasure chest of diamond rings; each one holding the memory of a life not lived, a road not taken. Maybe I was wrong, but it is too late to change things. My philosophy has always been: "You in your house, me in mine, and God in everyone's house."

And now this.... Here I am like a little dog, alone, not knowing if I will live or die, giving those rings to people who will pawn them away; knowing nothing of the stories behind them. One more time, I raise my eyes to the skies and tell God:

"If you let me out of this place, I promise I will love freely, unconditionally. Please, oh, beautiful God, just let me out of here. But oh, God, how can I ever love again after being abused by that ghost? Oh, God, help me!"

Someone knocks at the door, I quickly cover my head and Romeo comes in.

"Hello, my love. Oh, I love how you wait for me…. Listen, we spoke with your family and your daughter is going to go out today to get the jewelry. You know what? I think we're going to let you go soon. But I don't want to leave you."

As he says all this he calmly covers my eyes with the blindfold, tying it over the cotton balls pressed against my eyes, then frees my hair, and starts to comb it with the little comb he always brings. Then he sits me down on the bed and takes my sandals off. I can't tell but it seems that he is kneeling at my feet. Yes, yes, there he is, and he takes one foot in his hand and starts to kiss it, from the tip of my toe down to my heel. I cannot believe it, but it seems that I am about to relive a nightmare. The worst nightmare of all.

"My love, I don't want you to go. Why don't we make a plan? I would love to be your chauffeur, your gardener, whatever you want, just let me be near you; I need you."

His tongue starts traveling up my leg, and he lays me down on the bed and says, "I'm going to tie your hands and feet so that you can feel that you are completely and totally mine—no complaints, no tears, just you and me."

He undresses me. Then he takes out a couple of handkerchiefs and ties my hands to the bed frame. He starts to lick my body, all over. My tears spill out from under the blindfold, and I can feel them roll down my cheeks. When he kisses my face and tastes the salty tears, he whispers in my ear, "My darling, don't cry, everything about you tastes so sweet, don't ruin it with those tears. I could get mad at you, but you know what? With you something incredible happens to me. I'm a heartless guy, much more of an animal than you know, but with you I'm totally lost; all I want to do is love you and protect you and fuck you."

With that, he takes me by force, saying, "You know I'm a man of my word. I just put on a condom. When I leave here, I'm going to leave it above the bed, like before, so that you can see I don't want to hurt you."

When he finishes, he asks me if it was good for me. How this lowlife can even think to ask such a thing is beyond me. This is a rape. *I despise you, disgusting vermin, I despise you.*

"Yes, Romeo," I reply.

"Will you let me sleep with you? I want to take off your blindfold. I want you to see me. I want you to kiss me and look me in the eye."

"No, I will never look at you, I will never look at you," I say as I break down, convulsing with sobs. He tries to calm me down, telling me not to worry, that he's going to leave so I can rest, that tomorrow will be a better day for everyone.

"Well," he adds, "it'll be a better day for the other guys—because today has been the best day of my life." He gets up and walks out of the room.

Alone, abused, feeling stained by something I cannot wipe away, for the second time I go to the bathroom to scrub the one thing that neither water nor soap can clean: my dignity.

TIME

Time is the sphere of what surrounds the world.
—Pythagoras

Another day inside this new life-death. Breakfast arrives, and they turn on the television and radio as loud as they will go. I can hear some street vendor outside selling panties, someone else selling ice cream. Lying down on the bed, I look up at that goddamn ceiling with the plaster moldings that has become imprinted in my brain. Hours later, I pace the room in little circles, the size of my feet. Meal time comes and goes, and some semblance of daily life unfolds, always with the fear that never fully goes away; but it's odd, even fear itself has a way of getting monotonous.

I start to think about time. For Aristotle, time is a measure of change with respect to the before and after. What change was Aristotle talking about, internal or external? How can you measure time if you can't tell the difference between night and day? I think time exists only in the soul. It's like what St. Augustine said: how can the future diminish or exhaust itself when it doesn't even exist yet, and then how can the past, which is no longer with us, be something that grows? Because when you refer to the present, that present no longer exists. Only in the soul can past, present and future coexist. There are only three possible presents: a present of things past, a present of things present, and a present of things future. If you cannot conceive of the two others in the present, then none of them can exist. Here, in this place, if I do not bring to mind my childhood, it will not ever appear because it is part of the past. But if I remember it now, I will give it new life. And the same is true of the future; from the here and now I may design it and invent it, and in my future-present it will become a reality for me.

Time, in the end, is an infinite succession of moments. In captivity, I am growing less and less able to believe in time. But I still can't help wondering, how much of it do I have left?

Suddenly I hear a noise and I break out of my reverie.

Rudy knocks on the door and comes in with Cuquito. This isn't normal. Cuquito usually just comes in to pick up the dishes from the meals and then leaves alone, always alone.

"Hi, Sodi. We want to talk to you. We're really bored. How about you?"

"Of course I'm bored. There's nothing to do here but wait, and you know what they say, 'he who hesitates is lost.'"

"Look…oh, I'm so stupid, you can't see…here, we brought you a *churro*."

"A *churro*? What's that?"

"Ha, ha…oh, Sodi. A *churro* is a joint, you know, marijuana. Look at the nice present we brought you."

They light it and I begin to feel a bout of diarrhea coming on.

"No Rudy, I hate drugs. Don't give me drugs."

"Oh, don't be such a pussy…come on." They stick the joint between my lips, but I turn around and put my hands over my mouth to get them to stop insisting with their damn joint.

"This will really make the kidnapping a hell of a lot cooler. You start to fly and you'll forget all about why you're suffering so much."

"Hey, but what if she has a bad trip? Titi's scared, and a bad trip sucks shit."

"Yeah, I know, but she's gonna like it. Sodi, promise us you'll try it before you leave. We're just going to give you a few tokes. OK?"

"All right," I say, thinking that I'd rather die before doing drugs with these lunatics. "But first I want to tell you a story…."

"All right, Sodi. What's it about?"

"Once there was a man…he was very ambitious and very vain, and he wanted to live his life completely untouched by the effects of time. He wanted to never to grow old so that he could amass a great fortune, taking advantage of the people around him as they grew old and died. So one day, he met with the devil, who told him that he could grant this wish. The devil painted a portrait of the man, and only this portrait would bear the signs of aging, showing the effects of all the years lived and all the man's actions. Thrilled, the man began to wield this power, and the people in the city where he lived were shocked and amazed because he simply showed no signs at all of aging, and he never got sick. He could be wounded in a battle and not feel any pain; and this allowed him to kill his enemies off and, almost always, take advantage of the situation and collect their fortunes. Of course, he did do charitable things once in a while, but it was only to keep people from gossiping and to convince them that he was an honest and good man. His interest in others was just an act. When it came to love, he seduced young girls and married women alike, and he betrayed or abandoned them all. He collected them like trinkets. He seemed immortal, and he cared about nothing and no one at all. But his face was always a kind of expressionless mask; the mask of a man in love with himself, and he always wanted to show it off to the world. He hardly ever bothered to look at the portrait that he kept hidden in the basement—he kept it there out of sight because right from the start, the portrait had begun to show the very gruesome marks of all the things its owner had done. By this time, the portrait had changed so much that it no longer resembled the man at all anymore. His entire face was like one big festering sore, like a leper. And, if you could have smelled that portrait, it would have reeked of rot and decay. Somehow, one day, somebody discovered the man's secret—no doubt someone who had been harmed by him, or whose family, or sister, or wife had been hurt by him. One night, this person snuck into the basement and set fire to the portrait. Just then, the owner of the portrait came in, and his face began to undergo a transformation. As if by magic, the portrait slowly began to return to its original state, recovering its colors and features, while the man's face began to take on the grotesque form of his putrid soul."

"Come on, Sodi...that's worse than a bad trip. Let's just get out of here," he says to Rudy, and they leave the room which now stinks of marijuana. I can't do anything to get rid of the smell, though, and I have to sleep with it all night long.

The next day, I can hear a party going on somewhere near the house. It's very close by, and I can hear the band playing; it sounds like its right next door. There is live music, and the master of ceremonies makes all kinds of jokes. Romeo comes in and asks me if I want to go to the party. He really wants me to go, and he tells me that I can just put on a wrestler's mask, and nobody will recognize me. It will be so much fun, he says, to go out and dance a little.

Every time something like this happens, I start to go crazy all over again. Yes, yes, I know I keep using that word, but that is exactly how I feel when these totally insane things happen: that I am going crazy. Then I think to myself, wait a second—if I say yes, then maybe at the party I'll have a chance to escape, and then I can run away and get help, or else I can go into someone else's house.

"Titi, I know what you're thinking, but you can't escape—if I even take you at all. Don't forget, the first safe-house where we took you and your sister is just five minutes from here. That gives you an idea of things. Our group practically owns this neighborhood. And we never go anywhere without our sharpshooters...no, no, now that I think about it, I can't take you with me. Something bad could go down, and I don't want that. The guys would never forgive me, and maybe.... All right, my love, I'm leaving. Be good and don't do anything you'll regret later on. Just think about your daughters."

The bastard starts laughing, and he keeps on laughing as he closes the door behind him, because he knows he's said the magic words to keep me under control.

The noise is infernal and here I am, alone with Rudy, who has come in to collect the dishes from dinner; two sweet rolls and milk.

"You want something else?"

"Can you bring me some tequila and cigarettes?"

"Oh, so Sodi wants to party, too! OK, I'll do it, just don't make any noise, and you have to go to sleep early."

"OK."

He brings me the tequila and, amazingly enough, he also brings me an entire pack of cigarettes, which I gratefully accept like it's a priceless treasure. Smoking is one of the few ways I have to sooth all the anxiety and desperation I feel.

I ask him for the radio because I am determined to have a good time tonight. He brings me his black boom box, which has a broken antenna and a little pink bow tied onto the handle. When he leaves, I turn on some classical music, pour some tequila into a plastic cup, and light a cigarette. It is the most incredible moment, for I no longer hear the party outside, I am no longer scared and I actually begin to feel content. Yes, how strange—I feel happy. The tequila is Cabrito, and ever since my release, every time I drink that particular brand of tequila it brings me back to this night. The music playing is the opera *Prince Igor*. This is the first time I have ever heard it, and after my release, I look for it and it becomes one of my favorites. After a little while and a lot more tequila, I have had enough classical music. I want something happy, so I turn off the radio and sit there drinking and smoking with the party going on next door—or who knows, maybe the party is right here in this house. That would really be crossing the line, even for these sickos. At the end of the evening, I dissolve in tears, I fall, I laugh, I drag myself around the room and finally I fall asleep.

The next morning, all of us have hangovers. I hear bathroom noises, and some vomiting—that's Pancho— he's always throwing up, because he's always either drunk or hung over. I am suddenly overcome with a terrible feeling of guilt. How could I have been so irresponsible? How could I have done that, knowing that I was putting myself in danger? They could have come back drunk and abused me, and I would have been completely unable to think fast enough, to make any kind of decision for myself. Lucky for me, nothing happened. I feel depressed. That's normal, I suppose, after drinking a lot of alcohol, but I also feel scattered, fragmented, but I guess I deserve it…. Oh, well, I tell myself, don't punish yourself, it was a good way of flushing out all that pus that's been festering in my ravaged soul.

There's a knock at the door. I cover my head with the blanket and Rudy comes in. "Good morning, Sodi. How do you feel? God…did you ever make a mess, how much did you smoke? The boss is going to hear about this. Now cover up good because I have to let some air into the room, it stinks like hell in here. Listen, I brought you a couple of aspirin; they'll do you good. Nobody's going to bother you today. Today, the house is full of the living dead; they're all in just as bad a shape as you."

When I hear him comparing them to me, I get even angrier with myself.

"I was supposed to have the day off today but, well, I mean, look around. I can't leave if the other guys are all sleeping. And don't even think for a second that because I'm alone you can try and escape. I'm alone with an AK-47, two vicious dogs, and a grenade that I'll throw at you if you try to run, so you better just drink a little water and try to go back to sleep."

Kicking the door open, he exits the room and I take the aspirins, ruefully reflecting on how these demons seem to be able to read my mind.

In the afternoon, Romeo comes around. He is in a good mood, and he sits down next to me, in the little corner where I wait and wait.

"You know what, Titi? We all worship the Holy Lady of Death. She protects us from everything bad that could ever happen to us in this line of work. Almost all of us have her tattooed somewhere on our bodies. My tattoo is huge, and it's very beautiful. My White Maiden and my Holy Lady of Death are right here on my arm. Everyone respects and honors her in our neighborhood, and on the side of the building at the corner, there's an icon of her inside a little glass case. In her right hand she holds a scale, and the bony fingers on her left hand hold a globe. Her body is pure bones, all covered up in a long dress. And in front of this little altar there are lots of candles, and all around her are apples and cigars, glasses filled with tequila, beer cans and lots of other offerings.

"There are many people who worship the Holy Lady of Death. One of our neighbors has a little store right in his house, where he sells her in all sizes, for anything from one or two pesos, up to a hundred and eighty pesos.

"They say she's like a saint—she's the saint of evil people but she's also the saint of the poor, and the drug traffickers, of course. She's our mother, the mother of the kidnappers, and of all the people who sell stolen goods and pirated CDs in the markets. People ask the Holy Lady of Death for things they could never ask of the Virgin of Guadalupe, for example, 'I'm going to rob that bank; protect me.'

"The kids beg her to bring back their parents who are in jail. And Titi, the altar of the Holy Lady of Death is covered with flowers; lots of people make special trips to the neighborhood to say the rosary in front of the altar. Some people carry huge baskets of flowers on their heads, other people bring their own little figurines so that they can be blessed in front of the altar. The taxi drivers cross themselves when they drive by. And it isn't superstition; the Holy Lady of Death really exists.

"They say that our Lady of Death is pleased when the people speak of her with affection, using one of her favorite nicknames, like 'The friend' or 'The pretty lady' or 'the slender lady' or 'the noble lady' or 'the little girl.'

"This is one of the prayers we recite to her:

"*Blessed Death of my heart, never leave me without your protection, and never let so-and-so have a single minute of peace, bother him always, torture him, trouble him, trouble him so that he will always think of me. Amen.*

"After that, we say three Our Fathers, and then:

"Oh, holiest, most glorious and most powerful Lady of Death, you who are watching over me, in death, Lady, remember me, and do what I ask you at this moment, think of me and come to me, Holy Lady of Death, like the invincible Lady that you are. Please grant my wish and make so-and-so unable to enjoy anything without me, not eating nor sleeping unless at my side; so-and-so's thoughts shall be for me and me alone. Please give me the happiness that comes from that love. Amen."

"Oh, Romeo, you haven't prayed to her to cast something over me, have you?"

"I will never answer that question."

I am stunned at how these people have managed to juxtapose the worlds of the sacred and the evil. Their value system is so warped that they don't even know who to pray to anymore—God, Death, or the Virgin of Guadalupe. But they have to believe in something and their subconscious seems to be telling them that they are far, far away from God, because nobody who disfigures, dismembers and kills people can be close to God. And so they have created their own religion, totally removed from any other. They have no ethics. They cannot seem to understand that goodness is what brings happiness; goodness is what brings pleasure; goodness is living for others.

God help them.

PHASE THREE

THE RELEASE OR THE FINAL OUTCOME, THE POSSIBILITIES OF WHICH ARE MANY

FREEDOM

Freedom is nothing more than the spontaneity of the heart.
—Martinetti

I am sure they are going to let me go this week. I have been here for thirty days already, and I am constantly asking them when I will finally be released. Soon, they always say. Soon. But one day the Midget suddenly appears in my room, and tells me, "We're going to let you go, Sodi. We're not satisfied with the ransom, but this has gotten ugly. I mean, we either kill you or we let you go. They know too much out there, and the police are already looking for you. Today we're going to rehearse the trip to the place where we'll meet the guy who's handing over the money. And we all better pray that it goes off without a hitch because this is the hardest part of any kidnapping. If anything goes wrong, it all stops here. So get on your knees and start praying that your family acts as careful and cautious as they can be."

He leaves. I am trembling with joy because finally, finally I see a tiny sliver of light out of that hell! Oh, my God! Leave, I want to leave this place and see the sun, I want to breathe and hug my daughters.

"Our Father, who art in heaven...."

That night, Romeo shows up. He knocks on the door, and I cover my head with the towel. He comes in and says, "Hello, my love...I love how you wait for me."

"You know I don't 'wait' for you. Why can't you understand I'm locked up here; I'm here because I can't go anywhere?"

"All right, all right, you don't have to get nasty. We went and did a practice run today, to the place where the money will be handed over. We're a bunch of geniuses, you know that? You can't even imagine what we're going to do to the guy who hands over the money. They'll never be able to follow us; they won't find the tiniest little trace of us. We're going to let you go on Saturday. We're working out the details with your family right now. But I'm sad, because it means we're going to be separated. By the way, Rudy told me he offered you pot and you refused, but that you promised them that you would try some. Now, I forbid you from doing that, do you understand?"

"Well of course I wasn't going to smoke any pot, I just couldn't figure out how to get them to stop bothering me about it. I actually told them a story to get their minds off it. They were really, really stoned."

"All right, but you know that everything you and I talk about has to stay between the two of us. Now, I'm going to go out and buy you a red dress and a beautiful pair of shoes so that we can have our own little goodbye party. I want you to always remember me. And I want you to make me a promise. When you're back out there, I want us to see each other, so that we can figure out if what's between us is really love."

I am flabbergasted. I say nothing. Of course, there is no way I am going to tell this idiot that his perversity is only surpassed by his stupidity. He keeps talking:

"Listen, just so you don't forget, you were kidnapped on September 22, and now we're in October. But see, I am going to invite you, on November 22, to Bellini's, the restaurant at the top of the Walter Center. There, at that restaurant, you'll find me out in the open, so you can look me in the face. Now, I'm warning you, it isn't going to be easy to find me, and I'm going to be real careful, just in case you decide to change sides and work with the police. I may be with one or more women, and you will never know who I am. I'll be able to see you from where I'll be—not at a table or anything like that—and I will only walk up to you once I'm sure you're alone. Anyway, I can do a lot of things, don't worry about that; but the point is that you don't forget our date. And we'll drink champagne and we'll look out over the city at our feet, like two people in love who just want to kiss all night long, who just want to be together. Then, we can talk, and you'll tell me how you feel, and we can start to make plans. And who knows, maybe we'll even get married. Can you imagine it? What would my mother say? And your daughters? Do you think they'd accept me as their stepfather? You know once you're out of here, they're all going to try and tell you that we're a bunch of ruthless murderers, but you of all people know that's not true— come on, I even saved your little pinky finger and I always gave you good food to eat. But the most important thing in all this is that I fell in love with you. And listen, I've got women all over me because they know I've got money and they always see me driving around in those beautiful cars…. And once you get a look at me in person you're going to see that I'm very good looking. So, you're not going to stand me up on November 22nd, are you?"

"Of course not, Romeo, what do you think? Of course I will be there."

At that, he gets up from the floor, takes my head in his hands, covered with the towel, and kisses me violently, as if trying to seal this pact—that we will see each other once again after all this is over.

Thank God the goodbye date never happens, because they have a lot of work to take care of before they can let me go. And finally, the blessed 26th of October arrives. That morning, everything in the house is total chaos. The day starts at six-thirty. We all have to be up. Rudy comes in, waking me up with the television at full volume, and says, "Listen, you have to get washed up now. You're gonna have to be blindfolded all day long because we'll be coming in and out of here all the time, asking you stuff and getting everything ready."

"Are you going to give me back my bag and my clothes? So that I can go home dressed properly?"

"What are you, kidding? We gave that stuff away a long time ago. What you should be worried about right now is getting out of here alive. Now, I want to thank you for your sister's ring. But you didn't tell anyone, did you?"

"No, Rudy. Not even Romeo...."

"All right, Sodi. You know we're going to miss you. The best thing about you was all those stories, they were such a trip.... If all our hostages were like you, this business would be a hell of a lot more fun, 'cause then we wouldn't get so bored all the time.... Anyway, we're all of us now getting dressed for work. Every time we pick someone up or hand someone over we get dressed in black. Some of the guys even put on a suit. I don't. But we're all real professionals. And the plan; let me tell you, it's perfect. We're all going in different cars—just in case someone gets tailed we've got backup. I hope everything comes off all right and that tonight you'll be hugging your girls. I can see you love them like crazy. All right, Sodi, the hot water for the shower's ready. You just be very careful and keep the blindfold on at all times, OK?"

"Yes, Rudy. All right."

I can hear them go up the stairs, down the stairs,

start their cars, turn them off, I hear the dogs rustling around, and I think about how they forgot to bring me breakfast. At least I have some bottled water and some chocolates that Pancho gave me the other day.

At ten, Romeo comes in and I sit up in bed. Since I am blindfolded, I turn my head toward the sound of his voice.

"Darling, we're going out for the money now. This is the first time we've done this during the day, but the boss says that this way we'll really drive the police nuts— if there are police, that is. We're supposed to meet at noon. I love you. Wish us luck."

"With all my heart I wish you the best luck in the world."

He leaves. An acute, uncontrollable fear begins to take over my body. My jaw begins to tremble, and my teeth begin to chatter so loudly that I can no longer hear the noise from the TV set. Time passes by slowly; very slowly. Suddenly someone kicks in the door, which sends my chattering teeth into overdrive. It's the Midget.

"Who the fuck is Arturo?"

"What Arturo?"

"One of your sisters' boyfriends."

"Oh, yes, yes, sure, I know him."

"That piece of shit is the one who's going to leave the ransom. I pray he isn't an idiot and I hope he does exactly what we tell him to do. If not, he'll be the first dead guy on our hands. And I want to tell you something else…two new guys are going to stay here. You don't know them and they don't know you. They're sharpshooters who come only when we hand over a hostage. They've come from up above to see the money and take their share. But if something goes wrong, they'll come in here and shoot you in the head in a second. For them, you're just one more. When they come in to question you, you just answer whatever they ask you, don't say anything else. Understood?"

"Yes, sir."

"They're real animals, so don't make a fuss or even move when they come in. And don't say I didn't warn you. They're a couple of fucking dogs, those two."

He leaves. I don't know why but I suddenly feel so tired that all I can do right then is try to calm myself down by curling up in bed. And I fall asleep right away.

After a while—I don't know how much time—a rap on the door wakes me up and a pair of hands pick me up so violently that I urinate instantly. These are men I don't know. Their voices and their odors are new to me.

"All right, bitch, what was your favorite doll called when you were a little girl?"

"What? What? Oh, Ricitos."

They push me into the bed and leave with a thunderous kick to the door. I can hear them talking on the phone and swearing. The voices of these men send a chill up my spine. I figure they must be the right-hand guys of the big boss of all these different teams of organized criminals. They must be the ones who go for the money, and then divide it up. I also sense that they have added more cars and more men to today's operation. This means, then, that the people I know are only the tip of the iceberg of this army of criminals.

I am always amazed by how well-organized these people are, with their timetables, duties, roles, all neatly divided up among themselves. And I eventually conclude that if everyone in Mexico worked like these people do, but for good things, we would have a first-world country, no doubt. If we all worked together honestly, with care, dedication, discipline, and most of all with love for our wonderful country, I think Mexico would make great strides and would truly shine with all the natural blessings it already possesses.

Right now, however, I am paralyzed with fear. These fiends are murderers, I am sure of that, and my body hairs know it, too; they stand at attention like never before. These are the longest hours of my life, they drag on for centuries. Finally I hear cars and more cars pull up, and then I hear voices—around ten, maybe more. They all go out to the patio, and I can hear them pouring something. They move around, laughing and toasting one another.

"Cheers! Cheers!" they shout.

Two hours later Romeo taps at the door.

"Hello, darling. Everything went fine. But that Arturo sure is a dipshit. Would you believe he got lost three times? His face was white as a ghost, and he was sweating from his armpits all the way down to his hips. But it's all over now. The boss wants us to wait until night time to get you out of here, so that no one gets into any trouble. You know I didn't take my cut, right? Remember how I told you that I made a deal with them the day they wanted to chop off your finger? Well, today the boss reminded me of the deal we made and he didn't give me a thing. And they were all overjoyed, because they got more money. But I don't care; what I care about is that you're all right. Did you get something to eat?"

"No, Romeo, I haven't eaten anything yet."

"Oh, my God, baby, right now I'm going to get you something to eat, and then I'll come to say goodbye."

After a few minutes he brings me a sandwich and a soda, and he sits down next to me to help me eat, placing the straw between my lips. Then, when I finish, he leans me back and begins caressing my breasts with desperation.

"Oh, please, Romeo, can't you just leave me in peace already? Enough."

"Shh, shh…come with me, baby, we have to have our farewell—but it won't be for forever, will it? Wait a second, I have to go and get the condom and some mints."

He returns almost immediately, so happy with himself that he's singing:

"*Amor de mis amores, dueña mía de mi vida….*"

Laying me back down on the bed, he kisses me, and as he sticks his revolting tongue in my mouth, he slips me a breath mint. As he rapidly removes my clothes, all I can think is that they paid, that I am going to leave any moment now—I shouldn't have to go through this. My

God! The penetration is so violent that I am unable to hold back a cry of pain. At this, he puts his hand over my mouth and tells me he is sorry. This, more or less, is the last episode of terror that I am subjected to. Yes, this is the last one…there won't be any more, no more, I tell myself. Suddenly he turns me over and puts me on top of him. Ripping off my blindfold, he begins to shake like a maniac, and says, "Look at me, my love, look at me, I want you to see me when you have your orgasm." He starts making noises and I close my eyes tight. I will never look at this man, I think. Never. And this beast takes his pleasure. When he is through, he takes my face in his hands and covers it with kisses as I squeeze my eyes tighter and tighter. There is no way I am going to make that mistake; everything is paid up, the agreement is sealed. There is no way I am going to fall for this lunatic so that he can come back and tell me that he can't let me go because now I know what he looks like. With my hands I search for something to cover my eyes, and I find the blindfold, which I put on as best I can. Finally, I can rest.

"I can't let you go."

These words make me freeze. I am unable to move; my heart stops.

"Please, Romeo, don't say that!"

"I can't let you go. Listen, I was thinking about it this morning. I'll take you to my house and I'll keep you there like a little doll. I'll take care of you and give you everything. All I'll have to do is put a little chain around your ankle so that you can move around the room but you'll have everything. I have enough money to give you the life of a queen, Titi, and every day I'll give you a bath and I'll rub lotion all over your body. I'll brush your hair. I know you like to eat well, and I'll give you everything you ask for. I already talked to the boss and he told me I could do whatever I wanted, that they already got their part. Whatever I want to do is my problem, he said, and if I get myself mixed up in some kind of trouble it's not their problem. Only if it starts interfering with my work will I have trouble. So come, my darling, come with me."

"Please! Please! Romeo, please let me go."

It makes me feel so sad whenever I think back to that particular moment in my life. Naked, raped, sobbing, and defenseless, I fall to my knees, grab the legs of that maniac and I beg him to let me see my daughters again.

"Romeo, please! Let me see my daughters again, I can't stay with you, I have to see my daughters!" With my head pressed against his disgusting shoes I beg him to let me go over and over again.

"All right, Titi, all right. Don't be like that. I just want us to be together forever. But are you sure you're going to keep our date?"

"Yes, Romeo, I promise you I will be there."

"All right. Now go take a bath; we've still got a few hours before we can go."

I bathe quickly; I don't even care about trying to scrub anything off anymore. They have already taken everything they could from me. But now, at least, I am filled with the hope of seeing my family. Romeo lies down next to me in bed and we watch television. Well, he's the only one watching since I am blindfolded again, and just hear the sounds without really hearing.

The Midget comes in.

"Ernestina, everything's ready. We're going to take you out in an hour. But we have to check your orifices to make sure you haven't stuck anything in there that could be dangerous for us."

"No, sir, please! Don't search me, I haven't put anything anywhere, I swear it!"

"Pancho will put on a pair of gloves and look you over to make sure."

"No, boss, she hasn't got anything in there, believe me. Let it go, I'll be responsible for her."

"All right, all right, but only because I have to get rid of her already. She's really whipped you good, you know that? I wonder what Lupe's going to say...."

When the Midget leaves, Romeo takes my hands in his and says, "Don't pay any attention to him. Lupe means nothing to me. You believe me, don't you?"

"Of course, don't worry. I know how you feel about me. That's why I know you're going to take me to a place where I'm safe, where I can call my family."

"Of course, my darling, I have everything figured out so that you won't have any trouble at home. And something else, too; if you keep our date, the next day I'm going to send you a car with bulletproof windows so that this never happens to you again...and so that nobody can rob you on the street, either, because all those guys out on the street, most of them aren't nice like us. And I want to take care of you; I want to make sure that nobody ever hurts you, my darling."

He takes me in his arms and doesn't let go until the hour of my release.

Finally the moment arrives. Finally they are going to let me go. All the men file in, except the Midget. Rudy gives me a hug, and then deposits a few things in my hands.

"Look, Sodi, I bought you some sunglasses and a little stuffed bear. I really got to like you. So good luck in life and take care of yourself."

Then, Cuquito says, "All right, Sodi, take care."

Pancho just coughs and gives me a friendly slap on the back. Romeo hugs me and says, "All right, darling, we're going to leave you now. We're going to take three or four cars just in case we have to switch. You're going to go in the back, completely covered up. We're not going to blindfold you. You're just going to stay covered up in the jacket, and when you get out of the car you're going to put it over your shoulders and you're not going to turn around, okay?"

"Yes," I reply. They take me downstairs on Pancho's back, and he says to me, "Relax, Titi, everything's fine."

They set me down in the back of a minivan and cover me with several blankets. I hear a garage door open and we head out to the street. The first thing I can feel is the sound of other cars. The men turn on music by Luis Miguel.

"Titi," Romeo says, "If a policeman stops us, you just tell them that you're drunk and that you don't feel so well; that we're your neighbors and we're bringing you home. When we get to the place where we're dropping you off, you're going to hug me like we're boyfriend and girlfriend. You're going to put the sunglasses on before you get out, and look down at the ground. We're going to leave you near a Sanborn's [department store], you can call your family from there."

After about half an hour we get there. I am soaked with perspiration from the blankets, the fear and the adrenaline. I pray with all my heart that this is really true. They take me out of the minivan and I keep my head low. The first thing I feel under my feet is grass, and I realize there's no pavement. Suddenly the fear begins to gnaw away at my insides again. Are they leaving me up in the hills somewhere? Are they going to shoot me in the back? God, dear God, have mercy on me....

As I think all of this, Romeo is hugging me like an infatuated boyfriend. Slipping my arm around his neck, he whispers, "Titi, when I leave you, you have to count to one hundred very slowly, so that we can go. Then you're going to take off the sunglasses and you're going to put the jacket on right, and you're going to go to the store I told you about. Don't turn around, because this is all over; don't make a mistake. I'm going to miss you so much, my darling. Goodbye."

He sits me down on a bench. I think, "this is a park, and I am sitting on a bench."

"Romeo, are we in a park?" I ask. But nobody answers. The ghost has finally left me, along with his goons, and I am...where am I? One, two, three, forty-two, eight...I can't count. After a reasonable amount of time I take off the glasses and I put on the jacket, and I try to fix my hair. It isn't until I lift my face that the first gust of air enters my being. Air—blessed air. I open my eyes and I see the night and the stars and I can breathe and I can see and I can hear and all I want to do is let nature caress my battered body and soul. Nature indulges me tonight, giving me the biggest, prettiest moon I have ever seen in my life. The air is pungent with the smell of fresh, wet grass and damp earth. And the stars...all the stars laugh along with me, blinking and saying, "Hey! You are free!"

Yes, I am free after...I don't even know how long. I turn around to try and figure out where I am and I realize that I was right. I am in a park somewhere. It's nighttime, and it's pitch-black. It's so dark that I'm afraid something will happen to me if I don't get out of here. Not far away, I spot a bunch of sinister-looking men. Instead, I stand up and make my way over to a clearing, where I see a couple kissing. After walking a distance that is greater than the space where I was locked up, I am able to take longer strides, and I can feel my legs thanking me for allowing them to stretch long and wide.

I approach the couple and quietly ask, "Excuse me, do you know where the Sanborn's near here is?"

As soon as they look up at me, they scream and run away from me, pointing the way to the Sanborn's. For a moment, I am frozen in my tracks. I don't know what is going on. I turn around and right away I see the street; people walking, the pavement, lights, voices, noise. I stand there a moment just listening to the voices that are so lovely, like all the other sounds of human life. I couldn't be happier. In a few minutes, it dawns on me that this store is only two blocks from my house. What nerve, they practically dropped me off at my doorstep. At the entrance to Sanborn's I see a police car, but I don't want to go inside, because I'm afraid they'll tell me I have to go with them and file a report. And all I want right now is to see my family. As soon as the patrol car takes off, I walk into the Sanborn's and go over to the magazine section. I ask the man behind the counter if I can use the phone. He tells me to use a phone card, and I tell him I don't have one. A man standing next to me offers his phone; by one of those odd twists of fate, this man, Max Morales, will become one of my greatest sources of strength in the days to come. As I reach for the phone, the manager, along with a security guard, walks over. He asks me, "What do you want?"

"I was just robbed, and I need to call home so my family can come and get me."

The man looks me up and down. I will never forget those eyes.

"But...my goodness, they took everything, didn't they?"

"Yes, sir; everything."

The expression on his face changes, and he takes me by the arm, over to where I can sit, and he offers me a cup of tea. All I want is to talk to my family. They give me the phone and I dial my number. Marisela, the woman who looks after my daughters, answers the phone.

"Mari, I'm free; can I talk to one of my relatives?"

"Oh, thank God, thank God, *señora bonita*," she says. "Where are you? I'm coming to get you right now, and Salvador, the driver, is right here. I'm going to call your family."

"They're not there?"

"No, Titi, no, but please, tell me where you are."

"At the Sanborn's on Palmas."

"We're on our way."

I hang up and sit there, thinking: where on earth is my family? My daughters? I try to remain calm, and I can see people staring at me, smiling at me as if they all know what is going on. I turn around to look in a mirror on a column and I let out a yelp of surprise when I see my reflection. That ghostly vision with the hair and face of a madwoman cannot be me. That woman with the vacant eyes cannot be me. That woman dressed in a pair of old, black-and-gray pants with orange sandals...I look like a drug addict, an alcoholic. My exterior reveals that my body has aged just like my soul. Now I understand why that couple ran away when I walked up to them; clearly my appearance suggested I was going to do something to them. Poor Ernestina, I said to myself. What happened to you? I don't recognize you at all.

PHASE FOUR

THE VICTIM IS REUNITED WITH THE FAMILY, AND EMBARKS ON AN EXTREMELY DIFFICULT PERIOD OF ADAPTATION AND RE-ADJUSTMENT

THE RETURN

I didn't recognize you: I've changed a lot.
—Oscar Wilde

When Marisela appears, I hug her and she takes me out of the Sanborn's. We are both crying.

"Miss Titi, your family's on their way, they should all arrive at the same time."

"Mari, oh Mari!"

The door to my house swings open and as I go inside, I feel a tremendous relief and an overwhelming need to cry. All the lights are on, but there is no one there. I sit down in my living room, light a cigarette and look around at my house, my home, my life.

I hear cars. I am still sitting, and all I want is to see my girls. The front door opens and I can hear them shouting, "Mamá, Mamá, Mamá!" My daughters, my daughters. I see them, and they see me. With cries and tears we hug each other tightly, and the hug expands when my mother, my sisters, my nieces and nephews, and my grandmother join in. In a big circle, we are all one again.

They ask me how I feel. I still cannot believe that I am actually free. One by one, I look at each member of my family. My little daughter Marina, who I thought was in Europe, is right next to me, smiling at me with her great big eyes, red-rimmed from so much crying. My Camila is holding on to me, clinging to my clothes as if she will never let me leave her side again.

My mother's tears and kisses, little by little, dispel the cloud I have been living under for so long. My grandmother blesses me over and over again. My sisters touch me and touch me with all the tenderness in the world.

And yet, despite all this, I am suddenly overcome by an unbelievable sadness, and the feeling is so strong that I ask my family to let me go out to the garden by myself for a few minutes, because I don't know what to do with the feeling, and I don't want to expose them to it right now. And so I go outside, over to the big tree with the great, protective shadow, the one I have spent so much time reading under. Today, right now, I feel that the tree is waiting for me to hug it, and that is exactly what I do: I wrap my arms and my body around that tree. And then all the madness and all the pain that I have felt over the last few weeks comes pouring out. I scream like a madwoman, hugging the tree, crying and screaming and screaming and crying. Never in my life have I screamed so much, with so much pain and so much anger.

But my scream is not alone. It joins with others that have waited a long, long time to emerge, and some of them are as old as the thundering scream of the rebel angels falling into the abyss; like the scream of God after He was left all alone; the scream of Adam, gazing upon the face of the sands of time in Eve's wrinkles; the screams of the walls as they were brought down by Joshua's people; the screams of the clouds crying; the scream of Christ on the cross; the screams of dying stars; the screams of the flesh; the screams of the soul.

"Stop screaming!" I yell, trying to hush them all, because the screams are deaf from so much screaming. And my wails are so loud that all the other screams die down.... And silence finally settles over my home and my heart.

My family watches me through the windows, each of them joining me in spirit. And I stay there, releasing everything pent up inside me; all the pus, blood, green bile.... After a while I don't know what it is, but it flows and flows. The cries and screams seem to go on for hours, until my daughters come out and hug the tree with me, grabbing my hands and saying, "Mamá, everything is all right now. We're together again."

"Yes, girls, we're together. You don't know how much I missed you."

I look up to the sky, give thanks to God, and walk back into my home to be with my family.

We all curl up in the TV room. My daughters give me a bath, and all the clothing I wore home is placed in plastic bags for the police. The water in my house feels like holy water that, at least in part, heals the wounds of my spirit as it flows.

My family wants to know if the kidnappers hit me or hurt me in any way. But this is not the time to make them suffer any more. It is a time to celebrate because we are together, safe and sound, all of us. So for the moment, I don't tell them about anything that I have been through.

My first big surprise is the huge picture of me on López Doriga's news report. And I hear the journalist tell viewers:

"Ernestina Sodi was finally released and is presently back at home with her family. They say she lost eight kilos, and that a full medical evaluation is still pending."

"Mamá," I ask my mother. "What is this? What am I doing in the news? What is going on?"

"Oh, Titi, everyone knew except you. Literally, this story went around the world."

"But…how did it happen?"

"We don't know, but the news got out right away, when your friends went to the police station to file their report. After they gave the police your names, when they heard your sister's name they realized what it was all about.

But come, darling, come, you need to rest; you're so thin, do you want to eat?"

"Yes, Mamá, I want to eat."

In a little while, people start flowing in; people who have worked at my house for over fifteen years come by to kiss me and give me the hugs that all of us human beings need to be happy. They bring me cakes and a delicious stew of chicken and vegetables. Magdalena, my beloved cook who I adore, says, "This stew will warm your heart. Eat it, it's good. Made with love."

All night long we talk and talk and talk. My sister Laura's memories of everything, what it was like for them on the outside, what it was like for me on the inside. My family stays in my house for just over two weeks; all of us there, together, eating, sleeping, and watching movies together. Even my sisters' boyfriends sleep over, which is a first for me—after my divorce, no man has ever spent the night in my house.

Sitting around my house, we all begin to talk about the experience we lived over those harrowing days, in between tears and laughter. I learn about what they went through during my kidnapping, and I begin to realize that they, too, were held hostage in a way. Everyone piled into the home of one of my sisters, waiting for the kidnappers to call. As they waited and waited, they wandered aimlessly around the house, wearing pajamas all day long. They were petrified, too, for they felt certain they were being watched, threatened. There were entire days when they just cried, screamed, or sat around, depressed. For the duration of the kidnapping, they were holed up in that house, victims of the same circumstance.

Nobody knew anything. Some days they ate pizza, sometimes French fries, or sandwiches all day long. But food was the last thing on their minds; they had no appetite. My mother tells me that she spent hours and hours looking up at the ceiling, waiting for news. My sister Federica, on the other hand, sprung into action so fast that she was the first person to talk to the people at the Agencia Federal de Investigaciones (AFI) who assumed the role of counseling them throughout the negotia-tions—first with Federica as the contact, then Laura. Both of them tell me how difficult and traumatic it was to negotiate my life with them. They were dealing with mentally disturbed people whose sole motive was money. The federal agents never left my family's side, which was an immense source of comfort for them.

The federal agents had advised my family to keep communication at a minimum even between family members, to prevent information leaks, and my sister Gabriela, not knowing how much money the family had, immediately began gathering as much money as she could and in fact raised a considerable sum. Thanks to the help of my younger sister, though, they didn't need to use that money. Words cannot possibly express how grateful I am to my sisters, how thankful I am for everything they did for me. Thank you, I tell them; blood of my blood.

Yes, we are different now, very different, tired, beaten—both spiritually and morally. But we are together and we can see and feel each other and we can cry and laugh at our misfortunes.

My first night at home is absolutely wonderful. After hugging and kissing my daughters and everyone else, after bathing and eating, I go to sleep in my bed. As my skin makes contact with those fresh, clean sheets that smell like home, my body begins to relax for the first time. Living without adrenaline is strange in the beginning. But my new life has begun. My daughters sleep with me. For the entire night, and for several nights after that, they both cling to my pajamas so that I won't disappear while they are sleeping.

Not long after this, I begin to study victimology. I soon discover that my daughters have suffered what is known as the Empty Nest Syndrome, which many children of kidnapping victims suffer. All of a sudden, these children are forced to face death, abandonment, and the absence of a mother or father. They are at a total loss as to what to do, or how to act when their parents suddenly disappear. They try to understand these emotions, but all they feel is a terrible void. They have been abandoned, and they are haunted by the possibility that their parent or parents may die. When they get their mother or father back, it is extremely important for them to undergo psychological counseling so that they can begin to recover the faith that the kidnappers have taken from them.

For weeks, the telephone rings and rings constantly. All my relatives, friends and even more distant acquaintances call, concerned about me.

At a certain point I look around, and feel that my house has become the Garden of Eden, with flowers everywhere, fruit and cakes parading before me with messages of love and hope and an overwhelming sense of solidarity. So many people come by that at a certain point I actually get tired of it all, tired of telling the same story over and over again. But that story is not the same story I write about now. At that point, so soon after my release, I was still not well enough, nor was I ready to tell the simple and full truth.

The dominant feeling during this period is one of emptiness, and a persistent need to cry, all the time, about everything. I can't help but wonder if the absence of all that fear and adrenaline has left me with an odd sort of void, one that isn't so easily filled. Fear is an emotion, an intense one, and adrenaline is a substance that the body generates. And their absence, for better or for worse, is irreparable. My body has become so accustomed to these sensations that now that I begin to live without them, I feel a kind of dysfunction. It is hard to imagine, hard to experience, difficult to admit. But that is the way it is for me right now.

My new life is not the same as the life I left behind. It is new, because I am a new person. I can't approach this life as if nothing at all happened, because everything happened.

With time, the news of my release and the furor surrounding it, die down. Everything and everyone return to their lives, to some kind of normalcy. And what kind of life do I return to? I can't leave the house with the same confidence I used to feel. I am very careful about everything I do. Where is my sense of freedom? Did it stay behind with my kidnappers? Did I leave my smile, my laughter on that ratty old mattress in that tiny, squalid room? In the aftermath of all that has happened, I find that I am searching for myself, trying to figure out who I am.

THE SECOND KIDNAPPING

Not what goes into the mouth defiles a man;
but what comes out of the mouth, this defiles a man.
—Jesus Christ (Matthew 15:11)

I find myself held hostage again, but by the media this time, who turn the tragedy of my kidnapping into a lurid carnival of gossip and speculation. For the first few weeks after my release, my house is literally besieged by reporters. This is more than my family and I can handle. None of us can leave the house. The reporters clamor up fences, snapping photographs through windows, keeping up their vigil day and night. At one point, one of them offers money to my neighbor Luis to go inside his house and take photos and videos. Some of them dress up as delivery boys carrying flowers. One of the worst episodes is when someone, a driver, goes out to buy food and several reporters take advantage of the opportunity to scurry inside the house, into my own living room, taking photos like crazy. Now, I understand that my family, for various reasons, is in the public eye in Mexico, but after an experience as traumatic as the one we have just lived through, this feels like an unbelievably savage invasion of our privacy and our pain.

Three days after my release, we have to make our statements to the police, so that reports can be filed and the police can begin their investigation. We are terrified, however, that one of the reporters is going to follow us to get a story. Obviously, this is a security risk, because the kidnappers have threatened us. They don't care that we are all free, they have made it very clear that if we report this as a crime, or try to mess with them, they will drive past our homes and throw grenades at us. This threat will remain a constant in my life, until finally, I leave my beautiful country. But today, we have to go to the AFI to give our statements. One of the agents comes up with the ingenious idea of putting us in the trunk of his car to get past the reporters. Since I am still in something of a state of shock, I agree to this. What an awful mistake. At first, when they put Laura and I in the trunk, I am fine. But once the car begins to move I instantly have a panic attack, and I am overcome by an oppressive feeling of claustrophobia. My breathing becomes labored and I start to scream, but the federal agents can't hear me, and I begin to lose control. My sister calms me down, saying, "No, Titi, don't be scared. We've been released, we're not being kidnapped."

When we get to the AFI office I am in a wretched state. They give me water to sip and then I have to sniff a bit of alcohol to get my bearings back. In the end, though, after this episode is over, we find out that as we left the house some reporter had planted a hidden camera behind some trees.

When I make my statement to the police I have to tell them that on top of being kidnapped, I have also been raped. I ask them if I can give my statement to a female prosecutor, and the agents look at me, perplexed. My request is ridiculous—impossible, they say. And so when I sit down to face the man who represents the public prosecutor, I feel frozen. In the most insensitive, inhumane manner, he fires questions at me, without the least bit of tact or sympathy. Was I raped? How many subjects participated? Were foreign objects inserted inside my body? The questions, painful and aggressive, go on and on like this until I am finally so indignant that I stand up and tell him that I can't decide which is worse, being kidnapped or being interrogated by him.

After this experience, I formed an advocacy group for kidnapping victims. One of our most important achievements has been making basic human rights the primary focus of these government agencies. When a woman like me has to tell her story, no matter how inconvenient it might be, she must be allowed to speak with a woman who will be sensitive to the kind of male aggression she has been through. It is extremely difficult to talk about these things with a strange man, no matter what his title or position. With a great deal of work and dedication, we were able to change this in Mexico.

Facing the reporters was a hell that unfolded gradually. They simply refused to leave us alone, to allow our wounds to heal. And they began to tell our story with blood instead of newspaper ink. After all we went through, we had to defend ourselves, as a family, against all the ridiculous and often cruel things that some reporters and media said about us. One radio announcer, for example, said that we had actually staged the entire kidnapping for publicity, so that I could sell some books and my sister could become more famous.

When I heard this, I telephoned the radio station and asked to speak to the announcer.

"Do you mean Ernestina Sodi, the one who was kidnapped?"

"Yes, sir."

"We have Ernestina Sodi on the line. Hello, Ernestina…how nice to hear your voice. How are you?"

"Well, how do you think I am after what you just said?" I replied. "I don't understand why you have to treat us so mercilessly. Don't you think there is already enough evil in the hearts of those kidnappers, to go around spreading rumors that are just more of the same? All I want to say is that hundreds of people listen to you, and you have an ethical and moral responsibility to be constructive, not destructive. You are a part of Mexico, and you have an opportunity to offer wisdom to your public, so that your listeners can hear something positive, and feel something positive. Because your work is sacred, it reaches the hearts of so many people. And if you have any doubts at all as to the nature of our kidnapping, I suggest you go to the Attorney General's office to request information. I doubt they will lie to you. For my part, I forgive you and I hope God keeps you in his care."

Then there was the magazine that made fun of our misfortune by publishing pictures of me and my sister Laura in clown costumes. I spent an entire day crying when I saw that, all thanks to the journalist who came up with that story idea. Sometimes I think that the media in Mexico have reached a point of no return, and they need to recognize that they are partly responsible for many of the things that are wrong with our country. I truly feel that this kind of yellow journalism has emerged as the result of the moral decadence of our age, and the members of the press must recognize this fact. They need to think about how the things they produce affect them, too, because when they leave their offices, when they go home, they too are citizens, just like the rest of us. And I think their determination to spread negativity will ultimately turn against them. I would like to see the press cover the news in a healthy, respectful, ethical way. This would be an important first step toward creating an atmosphere of respect and well-being in a country like Mexico, and in turn people might finally feel able to trust the legitimacy of the media.

Thanks to all the news coverage, on television and the radio as well as in magazines and newspapers, our case served to shed light on the kidnapping problem in our country. Before, everyone in Mexico knew kidnappings happened, but only in very specific cases did anyone ever pay attention to the problem. With our kidnapping, people all over the world suddenly became aware of our national nightmare, and my family and I came to represent this unhappy social dynamic. From that perspective, I think it makes sense that people reacted with fear, confusion, and all sorts of mixed emotions that they channeled through us, because they suddenly felt as vulnerable as we had been.

PHASE FIVE

THE VICTIM BEGINS TO WORK THROUGH THE TRAUMA. A TIME OF SIGNIFICANT CHANGES—EMOTIONAL, SOCIAL, PROFESSIONAL, AND FINANCIAL

ROMEO'S CAPTURE

Of all base passions, fear is the most accursed.
—William Shakespeare, *Henry VI*, part 1

Life goes on, and with a fractured body and spirit, I try to rebuild my life. It is so hard. After a few months, on the surface it feels like everything has returned to normal. The same activities, the same friendships...everything just as it was before. But really nothing is the same for me. A month goes by before I am able to leave the house and attempt to lead a supposedly normal life.

The first time I leave the house is for the debut of my book, *Los Pinos, ésta es tu casa*, about the history of Mexico's presidential mansion. It took me an entire year to write it, and it should have been published while I was kidnapped. But I present it now, and I learn that there is indeed truth in what they say; that work is one of the best distractions known to man. I am determined to keep working on all the projects that fell to the wayside during my kidnapping.

Only after my release do I realize who really loves me, and who doesn't, and never has. It's as if I died and then suddenly came back to life, and I can see that my return makes some people happy and others less so. Sometimes it feels like I actually died and everyone began to split up my inheritance before my body was cold. For example, while I was kidnapped, a "friend" came over to my house claiming that I had clothes of hers that she needed back. The people who work in my house very politely let her come inside, because they assumed she was a trusted friend, and she practically emptied out my closet. Jewelry mysteriously disappeared. Since I have already lost so much, it doesn't really matter to me anymore—what do I care about a few more baubles? This woman then has the nerve to try and see me after my release, and actually returns the clothing, saying that she thought it was hers at the time, but that she made a big mistake.

On the other hand, of course, I have many wonderful friends who called my house to tell my family that they were extremely concerned about us, and that they were sending money over to help out with whatever was necessary. Thinking very practically, they realized that with the lady of the house gone, who would pay for things like electricity, water, and gas for the car? This might sound bizarre but it is true. My family was far too preoccupied to worry about things like my house and my everyday bills.

I learned of the loyalty and sincerity of my closest friends, who constantly looked in on my daughters. There was my friend Gina, who always asked them if they needed money for anything at all, even the simplest things, sometimes even taking them out to the movies. Knowing how fragile they were, she gave them all the affection she knew they so desperately needed at that time. And there was my friend Ana, who spent hours and hours in my house cleaning, because she knew that when I came back I would want everything to look nice.

Despite all this, after my release I go through a totally unexpected, and extremely frustrating experience; I start to feel very hopeless. I no longer have the high energy and motivation my family and friends have always known me for; they used to laugh and call me the president of the "Join the Optimists Club." Before, whenever someone felt bad and needed a lift, they always turned to me.

Now, however, I feel nothing—it's as if everything simply and suddenly has lost all its charm and color. And speaking of color, I lost 70% of my vision while in captivity. This may have happened because of the beatings, or the adrenaline, or possibly because I spent so much time blindfolded.

I also experience a great deal of difficulty in terms of my physical self. For example, I absolutely cannot have any kind of sexual relationship. And I get an AIDS test every six months. The doctor tells me that it isn't necessary, that I am perfectly healthy. But I don't know; it may just be my way of somehow trying to rid myself of all the things that were done to me. Intellectually I know this is not possible, I could not have contracted anything in the intervening six months. But still, I want to be sure, I always want to be sure. And I continue to take the tests every six months, like clockwork. After a year passes, I have my eyes operated on, and when they take the bandages off, the first thing I see is the most brilliant shade of orange, and the reds and yellows are so intense and beautiful, that I can only sink to my knees and thank God for letting me see color once again. I had grown used to seeing everything in hazy opaques and in the dimmest shadows. This is a tremendous gift for me, and I think that it is after the operation that my spirits begin to lift.

My sleep patterns are quite irregular, and I often have nightmares about the kidnapping. My skin, incredibly, begins to peel, as if I have been overexposed to the sun for a very long time. This makes me feel like a snake, shedding my skin, and my new skin is like that of a newborn baby.

For a long time after my release, I also find that I am constantly distracted. I interrupt conversations with non-sequiturs and act evasively in general. Because of this, I go into therapy for rape victims and I learn how to live with this particular fact of my life. I soon realize that I am not the only one who has been through this, and thanks to this group I learn that this man did not strip me of my dignity, my honor. Those are things that are mine, and always will be mine. I lived through a terrible experience, but it is in the past, and the past is where it has to stay.

Hearing God's words is perhaps the most important lesson for me. And the advice that I decide to follow, no matter what, is this: do not let bitterness take root in your heart. Slowly, I have begun to understand that I have to let go of the poison of the past, that I am only hurting myself and that I have to learn to forgive if I want to truly be free. For this reason, I forgive my kidnappers, so that I may feel free. I do this. Thanks to God, I do this.

I begin to accept my identity as a victim, and I study a tremendous amount about victimology. I gradually meet other people who have been kidnapped, and we become a club of sorts, because nobody can understand us like we understand each other.

After a while I start to work toward creating a support center for crime victims, and in the process I become an expert on the topic. Now I give lectures and I have even offered support therapy for crime victims. I knock on many doors and I have the satisfaction of being one of the pioneers in the struggle to open support centers in Mexico for victims of all kinds of crimes. Despite all this, however, there are times when, all of a sudden, the fear strikes me again. And whenever someone approaches my car my heart starts pounding wildly as I think, *they are after me.*

One of the most healing therapies for me is swimming. Before I try it, a doctor tells me that water is one of the greatest elements we humans can use to cleanse and heal ourselves. And so I get into the water in the fetal position and the therapist holds me in her arms. Whispering to me as I float, she tells me that the hour of my birth is upon me, and as I am submerged in the water I feel that I am given the chance to be reborn. Under the water, I feel that finally my eyes can rest from gravity and my ears, from all the noise outside. A feeling of complete peace comes over me, and the silence is absolute. The sounds I hear under the water make me feel as if I am in a liquid maternal womb. And then, suddenly, I feel clean, so very clean, and this feeling becomes the most important thing in my life; to feel cleansed of all the pain that man inflicts on his fellow man. And I am born. I have been reborn. When I emerge from the water, the doctor says to me, "Breathe in the new air, because from this moment on you are a new person."

After that first session, I go swimming every afternoon. I don't know what properties water possesses exactly, but its effect on me and my recovery is remarkable. Perhaps it has to do with breathing. Two strokes and then I take a breath; three strokes and then I take two breaths. In the end, I realize that breathing is the harmony of life and soul, and water is what helps me find that blessed equilibrium between body and spirit.

Once again, I am able to have some kind of faith in mankind. Little by little, I start to make plans, identify goals, and feel excited about things I want to accomplish.

After a year has passed since my release, I get a phone call very late one night at two in the morning. It is the AFI agents, calling to see if I can identify some voices on the phone because they think they may have caught one or two of the men who kidnapped me.

I sit up in bed to hear the tape they are about to play. As I listen to the voice, I jump up immediately and say, "yes, yes, I recognize the voice. It's Romeo." The agents come to my house right away, and as they play the cassette, I assure them that the voice is most definitely Romeo's. There are lots of things a person can forget in life but that voice is something I will never forget.

Two days after they capture him, they summon me to identify him in person. And I go to see my kidnapper and rapist. I can't sleep at all the night before, and once again I am bombarded by the long-forgotten sensation of adrenaline rushing through my body. My body reacts instantly by sweating and I lose control of my bowels. God, dear God, give me strength!

The agents come to pick me up in a bulletproof van, and they take me to the place they have the men locked up. The police hold the criminals for forty days before sentencing so that they can get information from them about the organization, its followers, and its operational structure. I am shaky and tense when I arrive—I am about to see the face of the man who was every man, for the first time. From this day forward he will have a face. Who is that man who I both despise and yet feel grateful to for saving my finger...?

The attorney general welcomes me warmly, for he knows the bitter pill I am about to swallow, and he asks me if I'd like a drink or if I'd like to wait in a small room while they bring him in.

I ask to wait, and my legs begin to tremble as I sit in the austere little waiting room. In a short while they come in for me and lead me to a small room with a big window. Behind the window is another, smaller room with very bright lights. The attorney general says to me, "We are going to bring the subject in directly in front of you and we are going to make him talk, so that you can identify him. Now, don't worry, because he cannot see you. This is glass on our side, but on his side it's a mirror."

And there he is.

Suddenly I see him, behind the two-way mirror where I can see him but he can't see me. I raise my eyes and my stomach contracts. They place him right in front of the window. For the first time he is standing directly in front of me. He looks at me without seeing me. I am looking at him and I, of course, can see him without any problem. What do I see?

A stocky, surprisingly young man, with very curly hair. He looks much younger than his age or perversity would suggest. His expression is like an eagle that knows he will die soon. Everything about him reminds me of how I was one year ago when I was a hostage completely at his mercy, locked up, raped, beaten, terrorized, asking him, begging him not to hurt me any more. He is like how I was then, for the first time feeling the fear, terror and horror of facing the unknown. Now it is him, he is the one locked up, treated like a criminal; sweating, trembling, and afraid.

But I need to see him up close. I can't confirm my suspicions from behind a glass wall.

"Sir," I say to the Attorney General, "I would have to smell that man to be completely positive it's him."

"Are you sure?"

"Yes, sir. Very sure."

They walk me into the little room where Romeo is. They have him stand in a corner, facing the wall, so that he cannot see me. To tell the truth, at this point I don't even care if he can see me. He has seen me so many times already, and this is my moment of triumph. But the officers tell me that for security reasons they prefer it if he can't see me.

Looking at him up against the wall, bare from the waist up, and shaking like a leaf, I feel a sense of giddy pleasure and satisfaction. This evil man will never hurt anyone again.

Silently I move closer to him, and I lean in to sniff just between his back and his shoulder. Suddenly, the smell enters my nostrils in a gust and my stomach and my soul recoil, and my head and my mind. It's him. Yes, yes, this is the rapist.

When he senses me approach, he begins to fidget and rivulets of perspiration roll down his bare skin. That is just how I want to see him, like he saw me before.

"Is that you?" he utters, and then represses whatever else he was going to say, knowing that it will only be used against him.

He knows it is me, just as I know it is him.

I say nothing, but I have to look at his hand, because I had seen a tiny scar on it once, when he had touched me, standing behind me and groping my breast. That time I had managed to get a glimpse of that scar from under the towel draped over my head.

I take his hand. Yes, it is the same scar. Even if I hadn't seen it, I still would have known it was him, the man who stole my womanhood.

As I take his hand to find the scar and try to turn it around, his grip tightens around mine. I can feel the perspiration, the adrenaline coursing through his body. He knows this is a turning point in his life, because if I positively identify him, he will get forty years in prison for my kidnapping, forty years for my sister's kidnapping, and forty more years for the kidnapping of the Princess, plus twenty-five years for rape. To say nothing of any other victims who identify and testify against him. In other words, he will never be a free man again, until they take him to the morgue to be buried.

Suddenly I feel emboldened, and decide to do the one thing they have warned me not to do: I speak to him directly.

Very slowly I move closer and closer to his ear and, my voice dripping with sarcasm, I utter the same words that rang through my head all throughout my captivity:

"Romeo, I love how you wait for me...."

CONCLUSION

Life is thickly sown with thorns, and I know no other remedy
than to pass quickly through them. The longer we dwell on
our misfortunes, the greater is their power to harm us.
—Voltaire

I put my last words on paper while sitting in a café in New York City.

Perhaps life brought me here to complete this project, to learn about solitude.

I am far from my country, against my wishes. Why?

Because the last episode of this drama played itself out when I went to identify my kidnappers. There were consequences. Some of his relatives had the gall to knock on my door and leave a message for me:

"Tell the lady of the house to drop the charges or there will be retaliation. This is now a personal issue between her family and ours."

In two days, I moved to a new house and detached myself from everything that meant so much to me for so many years. I left my life, my work, and most importantly, all that I love: my family, my friends, my colleagues, and my beloved Mexico which I miss more and more every day. At some point, sometime, I will return to live among my loved ones and in my own country. But right now, life has led me here. Naturally I refused to drop the charges, and I had to leave my cherished Mexico for my own safety.

But after everything was said and done, the most meaningful thing I learned from this experience was this:

To forgive.

Forgiveness was what freed me from the bitterness that poisoned my soul and my body. This does not mean that I condone what was done to me. The act of forgiving does not diminish the impact of what happened to me. Nor does it imply that my aggressors were justified in what they did to me. Forgiveness, for me, simply means putting aside all the negative feelings that caused me so much pain and anger, and kept me from moving ahead in my own life. I think that the inability to forgive held me back for a long, long time. Resentment had me tied up in knots, and this inability to forgive poisoned part of my spirit.

Forgiveness is a commitment that I have to renew on a daily basis, because the renewal of forgiveness is the key to freedom. And I want to be free. Here in black and white. In letters and words, I call this out to the four winds of the universe.

I, Ernestina Sodi Miranda. In the presence of God, declare that I forgive you.

After this, when you find your way back, the baggage is lighter. Material things do not matter anymore.

Today, the things that matter to me are love, my daughters, passion, the sunset, the sea, the moon, the air, the night, friendship. And I am here to say that after this harrowing experience, my life is now fuller and more meaningful than ever before, for I am a free woman. And the more I distance myself from material things, the happier I am.

A POEM TO LIFE

My love for life is so great
It has room for the flood,
And the story of the flood
And the Bible
From Genesis to Apocalypse
Every last letter
From alpha to omega
My love for life is so great it holds everything and nothing
It holds truth, not lies
It holds happiness, not deceit
It holds certainty, not doubt
It holds life, not death
My love for life is so great
It encompasses everything
And every passing moment it grows deeper and deeper
So deep that nothing can hold it, clothes cannot cloak it
And it runs naked through the world
My love for life is so great
The sun, the moon, the stars, thoughts, and everything else
Easily slide inside it
My love for life is so great...

—Ernestina Sodi Miranda

ACKNOWLEDGMENTS

For each of the most important members of my family:

For my beloved mother Yolanda: I thank you for my life, for your love, and I only wish that I could replace all the tears you shed when we were gone with stardust from God.

For my grandmother Eva: All my tenderness, for my beautiful little grandmother who wore herself out praying, who rubbed her hands until they were nothing but skin and bones. Always remember that you are the little grandmother of all the fairies of the universe.

For my sister Laura: My Lala, I want to thank you for the chance you gave me to see how much I could love someone, through the love I feel for you. Thank you, for fighting so hard to get me released, safe and sound. I wish I could erase all the pain you went through, with the enveloping embrace of God's peace.

For my sister Federica: My beloved Fede, thank you for your strength, your fortitude, and my respect and admiration for you because you are indeed a daughter of

Christ. Thank you for opening your home, your smile, your prayers, and most of all your faith in our lord, Jesus Christ. For having possessed the clarity to take charge of the situation in the first few days after I was kidnapped, and for putting us in the hands of the right people. And I want to tell you that, I know God already rocks you in his arms.

For my sister Gabriela: My Gabita. My love for you is so deep, so different. We share so many memories, our adolescence, our sisterhood. Thank you! For your intelligence, and your example. I wish I could wipe away all the terrible moments that you lived through because of incompetence and misunderstanding. For you, all my affection and admiration. Always remember that your will is the essence of the golden Cosmos.

For my sister Thalía: My Thali, I dedicate this book to you with all the love that one sister can feel for another. Thank you! Because you assumed the financial responsibility of the situation from the very first moment. You were the one who told my mother that you would take care of the financial reality of our kidnapping, and that we would not die if this was a question of money. I would like to make it clear here that you were the one who paid our ransom. Thank you because I know the sacrifices you made and the obstacles you overcame to get us out. You have been the truest and most loving sister. My little big sister, I want to bring a smile to your face by giving you thousands of butterflies of all different colors, to refresh your soul and to turn those excruciating days of anguish into brilliant rays of sunlight, so that when they cast their light on you, you think of me, and of how I love you. Always remember that your light is the sweet honey of all that is good in the world.